PYTHON CRASH COURSE FOR BEGINNERS

A Thrilling Challenge to Python Mastery

Mark Reed & CyberEdge Press

Table of Contents

Introduction vii

CHAPTER 1: Entering Pythonia—The Valley of Variables 1

Introduction to Variables 1

    Example 1: Storing User Input 3

    Example 2: Performing Calculations 3

    Example 3: Using Appropriate Naming Conventions 4

Data Types in Python 4

    Integers 4

    Floats 4

    Strings 5

    Booleans 5

Arithmetic and String Operations 6

    Basic Operations on Numerical Data 6

    Manipulating Strings 7

    Displaying Output With the print() Function 7

    Gathering User Input With the input() Function 8

    Bringing It All Together 8

Type Conversion 9

Applied Variable Manipulation 12

Final Boss: The Return of the Variable Vortex 14

CHAPTER 2: Loops Lagoon 16

for Loops 16

while Loops 18

    User Input Validation 19

    Searching Through Data 19

    Game Loops 20

Loop Control 21

Conditionals 24

    Understanding if Statements 24

    Adding Complexity With elif and else 24

Combining Multiple Conditionals 25

Nested Conditionals for Harder Decisions 25

Loop Leviathan: The Final Challenge 27

CHAPTER 3: The Array Archipelago 30

Understanding Lists in Python 30

Indexing: Accessing Elements by Position 31

Common List Methods 31

Exploring Tuples as Immutable Sequences 32

Mastering Sets: The Island of Uniqueness 33

Confronting the Array Hydra 33

CHAPTER 4: The Dictionary Desert 36

Dictionaries: Your Compass in the Desert 36

Navigating the Dunes: Accessing and Modifying Data 37

Complex Data Structures: The Oasis of Nested Dictionaries 38

The Journey Through the Desert: Iterating Over Dictionaries 40

Iterating Over Keys Using a for Loop 41

Iterating Over Values Using the values() Method 41

Practical Applications of Iterating 41

The Final Boss: Confronting the Key-Guardian 42

CHAPTER 5: The OOP Labyrinth 46

The Gateway to the Labyrinth: Understanding Classes and Objects 46

The Hidden Passageways: Exploring Inheritance 48

The Labyrinth Walls: Encapsulation in OOP 49

The Shifting Walls: Harnessing Polymorphism 51

The Final Chamber: Confronting the Class Chimera 52

CHAPTER 6: The Debugging Jungle 56

The Jungle Underbrush: Common Syntax Errors 56

Tangled Vines: Missing Colons and Unmatched Parentheses 57

Hidden Pitfalls: Incorrect Indentation 57

The Camouflaged Threat: Misspelled Keywords or Variable Names 58

Exercises: Clearing the Path 58

The Quicksand of Execution Errors 60

The Sinking Feeling: Division by Zero 60

The Hidden Sinkhole: Accessing Undefined Variables or Out-Of-Range Indices 60

The Poisonous Plants: Inappropriate Data Types or Invalid Function Arguments 61

The Mirages: Logic Errors 62

The Importance of Testing 65

The Tools of Survival: Debugging Tools and Techniques 66

The Machete: Print Statements 66

The Compass: Built-in Debugging Tools 66

The Shield: Error Handling 66

The Final Chamber: Confronting the Final Boss: Error Entity 67

CHAPTER 7: The Function Fields 69

The Foundation of the Fields: Defining Functions With Parameters and Return Values 69

Planting the Seeds: Learning to Use the def Keyword 69

Nurturing Growth: Passing Parameters Into Functions 70

Harvesting the Crops: Understanding Return Values 71

Tending to the Fields: The Importance of Clear and Descriptive Function Names 71

The Fields in Bloom: Best Practices 72

The Boundaries of the Fields: Understanding Function Scope 73

Going Deeper: Recursive Functions and Lambda Expressions 75

The DRY Principle: Avoiding Repetition in the Fields 77

The Final Boss: Function Fiend 79

CHAPTER 8: The Modules Mountain 81

The Beginning of the Ascent 81

The Standard Library Trail 81

Venturing Into the PyPI Forest 83

Crafting Custom Modules 85

The Final Challenge: Facing the Module Minotaur 86

CHAPTER 9: The Data Marketplace 90

Entering the Marketplace 90

Setting Up Shop: File Operations 90

Exploring the Marketplace: CSV and Excel Files 91

Navigating the Data Bazaar: Pandas 92

The Final Boss: Facing the Data Dragon 94

CHAPTER 10: The API Abyss 98

Introducing APIs..98

Setting Sail: Understanding APIs 98

Navigating the Seas: Making Your First API Call.............................99

Deciphering the Message: Handling JSON Responses 100

Exploring the Depths: Real-World Applications of APIs...................100

Data Formats in APIs 101

Introduction to Web Scraping 104

Facing the Kraken: The Final Boss 106

CHAPTER 11: The Final Fortress 114

Exploring the Fortress..114

Challenge 1: List Comprehensions and Dictionaries........................115

Challenge 2: OOP 115

Challenge 3: File Handling 117

Challenge 4: API Integration 117

The Penultimate Challenge 118

Bugzilla: The Ultimate Challenge...120

Conclusion...128

References...132

Introduction

Right now, you're sitting in the comfort of your own home, with the hum of modern technology around you. You're curled up with your favorite device, perhaps a laptop or tablet, enjoying a quiet moment of peace. Suddenly, an unusual sight catches your eye—a small, glowing object on your desk. Intrigued, you move closer and discover that it's unlike anything you've ever seen before. It's an artifact, ancient yet emanating a strange glow. Little do you know, this is the beginning of an extraordinary journey.

The artifact whirs to life, displaying a message from a wise mentor named Py. Py hails from a mysterious land called Pythonia, a place where balance and order have been disrupted by the mischievous Bugzilla. Py explains that Pythonia's code—the lifeblood of their world—has been corrupted, and only someone with a fresh perspective and a courageous heart can help restore it. Py believes that person is you.

Welcome to your programming adventure! Whether you've been in coding before or you're completely new to it, this journey will open doors to a world filled with limitless possibilities. But before we dive into the depths of Pythonia, we need to prepare. Just like any great hero, you'll need the right tools and knowledge to succeed. That means setting up your very own programming environment—a space where you can create, experiment, and bring your ideas to life.

But first things first: let's talk about Python. This language is your key to Pythonia. It's versatile, powerful, and surprisingly easy to learn. To begin this wonderful adventure, you'll need to download and install Python on your system. Visit the official Python website, where you'll find the latest version. Make sure to choose the correct version for your operating system—whether that's Windows, macOS, or Linux. The installation process is straightforward, and soon enough, you'll have Python ready to go.

Next, every programmer needs a good integrated development environment (IDE). Think of an IDE as your workshop, complete with all the tools you need to craft your code. There are several great options available, each with its unique features. PyCharm, for example, offers a set of tools for professional developers, while Thonny is user-friendly and perfect for beginners. Then you have Visual Studio Code that has a balance between simplicity and functionality, making it another excellent choice. Whichever IDE you choose, it will aid you in writing, testing, and debugging your code, ensuring a smooth and efficient workflow.

Now that we have our environment set up, it's time for a little magic—your first Python script! Imagine the excitement of seeing your code come to life! Open your chosen IDE, and let's write a simple program. Type out the following:

```
print("Hello, World!")
```

This may seem straightforward, but it's a monumental step because you're not just typing words; you're commanding a machine to perform an action. Now, click the "Run" button, and watch as "Hello, World!" appears on your screen. Congratulations! You've just written and executed your first Python script! Easy, right?

But what lies beyond this initial triumph? Python is more than just a single script. It's a gateway to an extensive ecosystem bustling with opportunities. Nearly every industry you can think of uses Python in some form. In web development, Python frameworks like Django and Flask power countless websites and applications, offering dynamic user experiences. If data science piques your interest, Python's libraries such as Pandas, NumPy, and Matplotlib provide the tools needed to analyze and visualize complex datasets, uncovering insights that drive decision-making in businesses around the world.

Automation is another realm where Python shines brightly. From automating repetitive tasks to managing large systems, Python scripts can save time and reduce errors, increasing efficiency across various fields. Oh, and let's not forget about artificial intelligence and machine learning, Python's capabilities in these cutting-edge areas are supported by powerful libraries like TensorFlow and Scikit-Learn. As you can see, if you learn Python, you're opening doors to industries and careers that impact the world in many ways.

Now, let's stop with the formalities and start our adventure on Pythonia. But before that, remember that every line of code you write brings you closer to mastering these skills. The journey may have its challenges, but each obstacle is an opportunity to grow and learn. Along the way, Py will be there as your guide, providing wisdom and encouragement whenever needed.

"Hey! Don't forget about me!" a small voice pipes up, and you turn to see a tiny, charming robot waving energetically.

Oh, how could we forget? Meet Debugger, your trusty sidekick! This little robot isn't just adorable; Debugger is packed with practical knowledge and ready to offer concrete help whenever you hit a snag. With Debugger by your side, even the trickiest problems become manageable—and maybe even fun! Whether it's through a quirky joke or a handy tip, Debugger ensures that you never feel alone on your journey.

You're not alone in this quest—it's time to start and join a community of programmers around the world who share your passion for coding. Don't hesitate to seek advice, share your progress, and celebrate your achievements with fellow adventurers. Together, we'll face the complexities of code, unlock the secrets of Python, and perhaps even discover new realms of possibility.

So, take a deep breath and prepare yourself for the road ahead. With your programming environment established and your first script successfully run, you've already taken the first steps on a path that could change everything. Welcome to the world of Python. Welcome to your journey as a programmer. Let's go to Pythonia and see where this incredible adventure leads us.

CHAPTER 1

Entering Pythonia—The Valley of Variables

Now you're entering the world of Pythonia, and you quickly discover that the entire landscape is built upon variables. Just like ingredients in a recipe, variables are the building blocks of any program, holding and managing data that drives functionality and logic. Whether you're capturing user input, performing calculations, or storing text information, variables are the key components ensuring everything operates smoothly behind the scenes.

Introduction to Variables

Variables in Python serve as labeled containers that store and manage information within a program. In Pythonia, these variables are essential for maintaining and manipulating data throughout your code. For example, if you wanted to store the age of a user or the total price of items in a shopping cart, you'd use variables to keep these values.

Declaring a variable in Python is straightforward. You simply choose a name for your variable and use the assignment operator = to set its value. For instance, to store the number 25 in a variable named **age**, you'd write:

```
age = 25
```

Here, **age** is the variable name, and **25** is the value assigned to it. The = sign is not indicating equality but rather assigning the value on the right side to the variable on the left.

When naming variables, readability is crucial. Clear and descriptive variable names make your code easier to understand and maintain. Here are some examples:

1. **Descriptive names:** Use names that describe the variable's purpose. Instead of using single letters like **x** or **y**, opt for names like **user_age** or **total_price**.

2. **Use underscores:** In multiword variable names, use underscores to separate words (**total_price**), making them easier to read.

3. **Avoid reserved keywords:** Python has reserved keywords with special functions (such as **print, for, while**). Avoid using these as variable names.

4. **Keep it lowercase:** Variable names should generally be in lowercase letters. Uppercase letters are often used for constants.

Here's an example following these conventions:

```
user_name = "Alice"
total_items_in_cart = 5
```

Once a variable is declared, you can change its value anytime by assigning a new value to it. This process is known as reassignment. Continuing with our earlier example, you might alter the **age** variable if the user's age changes:

```
age = 30
```

After this line, the **age** variable will store the value 30 instead of 25. Variables can also change types over their lifetime. For example:

```
user_age = 25
user_age = "twenty-five"
```

Initially, **user_age** is an integer storing the value 25. After reassignment, it's a string holding the text "twenty-five". This flexibility allows Python variables to adapt to different kinds of data as needed.

To see how this works in a program, let's imagine building a simple script that collects a user's age and name, then reassigns these values to simulate a change:

```python
# Declare initial variables
user_name = "Alice"
user_age = 25

print(f"User Name: {user_name}")
print(f"User Age: {user_age}")

# Reassigning new values to the variables
user_name = "Bob"
user_age = 30

print("Updated User Information")
print(f"User Name: {user_name}")
print(f"User Age: {user_age}")
```

In this script, we start by setting **user_name** to "Alice" and **user_age** to 25. Later, we update these variables to new values, demonstrating how variables can be reassigned at any point in the program.

Let's take a closer look at some additional examples to reinforce these concepts.

Example 1: Storing User Input

You can use variables to store input from a user. This is especially useful for interactive programs:

```python
user_input = input("Enter your favorite color: ")
print(f"Your favorite color is {user_input}")
```

Here, **input()** captures what the user types and stores it in the variable **user_input**. We can then use this variable elsewhere in our program.

Example 2: Performing Calculations

Variables can hold the results of calculations, which is handy for various computational tasks:

```python
num1 = 10
num2 = 5
sum = num1 + num2
print(f"The sum of {num1} and {num2} is {sum}")
```

In this case, **num1** and **num2** store numbers, and the variable **sum** holds the result of adding these two numbers together.

Example 3: Using Appropriate Naming Conventions

Imagine writing a program to manage a book collection. By following good naming practices, you can keep your code organized and readable:

```python
book_title = "1984"
author_name = "George Orwell"
publication_year = 1949
price = 19.99

print(f"Title: {book_title}")
print(f"Author: {author_name}")
print(f"Year: {publication_year}")
print(f"Price: ${price}")
```

In the above code, each variable name clearly indicates its content, making the code easy to follow.

Data Types in Python

One of the foundational concepts to grasp is understanding and manipulating various data types. Data types in Python are essentially categories of data that dictate how the language interacts with them.

Integers

First, let's explore integers. In Python, integers are whole numbers without a decimal point. They can be positive or negative and are commonly used for counting and performing arithmetic operations. For example, if we want to count the number of apples in a basket, we'd use an integer. Arithmetic operations such as addition, subtraction, multiplication, and division are effortlessly carried out on integers in Python. Consider the simple equation 5 + 3. Here, both 5 and 3 are integers, and their sum is also an integer. The intuitive nature of integers makes them a useful data type for everyday calculations and logical decision-making.

Floats

Next up are floats. These represent decimal numbers, offering more precision than integers. This added precision is essential when dealing with measurements or calculations requiring greater accuracy. For instance, consider calculating the total cost of several items priced at $9.99 each. Using floats allows us to account for every cent correctly. In Python, performing arithmetic operations on floats is just as straightforward as with integers. However, it's worth noting that due to the way computers handle floating-point arithmetic, very large or very small floats might introduce tiny rounding errors. Still, for most applications involving money or scientific measurements, floats provide the necessary precision.

Strings

A string in Python is a sequence of characters enclosed within single or double quotes. Strings enable text manipulation, making them indispensable for tasks like storing names, messages, or any textual information. For example, the word "Pythonia" is stored as a string. Strings can be concatenated (joined together) using the plus operator (+), allowing you to combine multiple pieces of text. For instance, combining "Hello" and "World" results in "HelloWorld." Additionally, strings have powerful built-in methods that let you modify and analyze text efficiently. You can convert strings to uppercase, find specific characters, or even break them apart into smaller segments.

Booleans

Booleans, the final primary data type we'll discuss, represent binary values: True or False. Booleans are crucial for logical operations and comparisons. In Python, Booleans often emerge from comparison statements or conditions. For example, the statement 10 > 5 evaluates to True, while 10 < 5 evaluates to False. These evaluations are important in decision-making structures like if-else statements, controlling the flow of a program based on certain conditions. Booleans can also be the result of logical operations such as AND, OR, and NOT, providing a mechanism to build complex decision logic within your code.

To bring these concepts home, let's walk through some practical examples.

Imagine you're tasked with developing a simple budget calculator. You'll need to keep track of different expense categories, summing monthly costs, and evaluating whether they fit within your budget. Here's how you'd harness each data type:

1. **Integers:** Use integers to count the number of expenses in each category. If you have 5 utility bills, represent this count with an integer.

2. **Floats:** Represent the actual cost of each bill as a float. If your electricity bill is $45.67, store it accurately using a float. Summing these precise values ensures an accurate total expenditure.

3. **Strings:** Store descriptions of each expense as strings. Descriptive labels like "Electricity Bill" or "Grocery Shopping" make your budget calculator user-friendly and informative.

4. **Booleans:** Use Booleans to evaluate conditions, such as whether the total expenditures exceed your budget. If your budget is $1,000 and your total expenses sum to $1,050, a Boolean comparison (total_expenses > budget) will return True, signaling overspending.

Arithmetic and String Operations

Here in Pythonia, the Valley of Variables, you encounter a world where data is dynamic and versatile. Understanding how to manipulate this data is crucial for any budding Pythonista. To continue with our adventure, let's explore basic operations on numerical and string data, key functions like **print()** and **input()**, and how they form the foundation for more advanced programming concepts.

Basic Operations on Numerical Data

Arithmetic With Integers and Floats

Numbers in Python can be whole (integers) or fractional (floats). Performing arithmetic operations with these numbers is straightforward:

1. **Addition:** Use the + operator to add numbers.

```python
x = 5
y = 3
result = x + y
print(result)   # Output: 8
```

2. **Subtraction:** Use the - operator to subtract one number from another.

```python
x = 5
y = 3
result = x - y
print(result)   # Output: 2
```

3. **Multiplication:** The * operator multiplies numbers.

```python
x = 5
y = 3
result = x * y
print(result)  # Output: 15
```

4. **Division:** Use the / operator to divide numbers and get a float, or // for integer division.

```python
x = 5
y = 3
result = x / y
print(result)  # Output: 1.6666666666666667
result_int_div = x // y
print(result_int_div)  # Output: 1
```

These operations allow you to perform calculations and solve problems involving numerical data effectively.

Manipulating Strings

Strings, sequences of characters, are equally important in Python. Combining strings, or concatenation, helps in creating meaningful messages or outputs.

String Concatenation

To concatenate strings, use the + operator:

```python
greeting = "Hello"
name = "Alice"
message = greeting + ", " + name + "!"
print(message)  # Output: Hello, Alice!
```

This technique is particularly handy when you need to build dynamic text outputs.

Displaying Output With the print() Function

Displaying information to the user is one of the most fundamental aspects of programming. Python's **print()** function is designed for this purpose. It can display numbers, strings, and even combinations of both.

Example of Using print()

```python
# Printing a single item
print(100)  # Output: 100

# Printing multiple items
a = 5
b = 10
print("The value of a is", a, "and the value of b is", b)  # Output: The value of
a is 5 and the value of b is 10

# Using formatted strings
name = "Bob"
age = 25
print(f"{name} is {age} years old.")  # Output: Bob is 25 years old.
```

With the **print()** function, you can present your program's results clearly and concisely.

Gathering User Input With the input() Function

Your programs often need to interact with users by collecting input. The **input()** function reads a line of text entered by the user.

Example of Using input()

```python
user_name = input("Enter your name: ")
print("Hello, " + user_name + "!")  # If user enters 'John', output will be:
Hello, John!
```

You can also convert the input to other data types such as integers or floats if needed:

```python
user_age = int(input("Enter your age: "))  # Converts input to integer
print(f"You are {user_age} years old.")
```

Bringing It All Together

Combining these elements allows you to create interactive and functional Python programs. Here's an example that ties everything together:

Example Program

```python
# Interactive Calculator
print("Welcome to the simple calculator!")
num1 = float(input("Enter the first number: "))
num2 = float(input("Enter the second number: "))

addition = num1 + num2
subtraction = num1 - num2
multiplication = num1 * num2
division = num1 / num2

print(f"The sum of {num1} and {num2} is: {addition}")
print(f"The difference between {num1} and {num2} is: {subtraction}")
print(f"The product of {num1} and {num2} is: {multiplication}")
print(f"The quotient of {num1} divided by {num2} is: {division}")
```

Type Conversion

Converting data from one type to another is a fundamental skill that will help you solve many problems efficiently. Let's explore this concept by breaking it down into manageable chunks.

Firstly, let's talk about converting a string to an integer using the **int()** function. This process, known as type casting, is straightforward but essential when dealing with numeric data stored as strings. Imagine you have a string representing a number, like **'123'**. If you want to perform arithmetic operations on it, converting it to an integer is necessary. Here's how you do it:

```python
num_string = '123'
num_integer = int(num_string)
print(num_integer)  # Outputs: 123
```

In the example above, the **int()** function takes the string **'123'** and converts it to the integer **123**. Without this conversion, attempting to add or subtract this value would result in an error.

Now, let's illustrate converting a number to a string using the **str()** function. This can be particularly useful when you need to concatenate numbers with strings for display purposes. For example, if you wanted to create a message that includes both text and numbers, converting the numbers to strings makes it possible:

```
age = 30
message = "I am " + str(age) + " years old."
print(message)  # Outputs: I am 30 years old.
```

Here, the str() function converts the integer 30 into the string '30', allowing it to be concatenated with the other string parts.

Understanding why and when to use type conversion is crucial. There are many scenarios where type conversion is necessary. For instance, data received from user input via the input() function is always considered a string. If a user enters a number you're expecting to perform calculations with, converting this input from a string to an integer or float is necessary. Consider this scenario:

```
user_input = input("Enter a number: ")
number = int(user_input)
doubled_number = number * 2
print("Your number doubled is:", doubled_number)
```

In this case, the user input needs to be converted to an integer so that the multiplication operation can be performed correctly. Without the int() conversion, Python would raise an error because you're trying to multiply a string by an integer.

Beyond simple conversions, typecasting allows you to avoid common errors and make your code more robust. By explicitly converting data types, you ensure that your program behaves as expected. Let's look at another example to drive this point home:

```
salary_str = "50000"
bonus = 5000

# Attempting to add without conversion results in an error
# total_income = salary_str + bonus  # Raises TypeError

# Correct way with explicit conversion
total_income = int(salary_str) + bonus
print("Total income:", total_income)  # Outputs: Total income: 55000
```

This example shows the necessity of explicit type conversion to avoid errors. Initially, trying to add a string (salary_str) and an integer (bonus) throws a TypeError. However, converting salary_str to an integer ensures that the addition is performed correctly.

There are situations where Python handles type conversion implicitly. This typically occurs when there's no risk of losing information. For example:

```python
integer_number = 10
float_number = 5.5
result = integer_number + float_number
print(result)  # Outputs: 15.5
print(type(result))  # Outputs: <class 'float'>
```

Here, Python automatically converts the integer to a float before performing the addition. This implicit conversion ensures precision is not lost, as floats can represent decimal values while integers cannot.

However, relying on implicit conversions can sometimes lead to confusion and unintended behaviors. It's generally good practice to use explicit conversions through functions like **int()**, **str()**, **float()**, and so on, to make your intentions clear and your code easier to understand.

To further solidify your understanding, let's consider a real-world scenario using a dictionary and tuples. Suppose you have a tuple containing key-value pairs and you need to convert it into a dictionary for more efficient data handling:

```python
data_tuples = (('name', 'Alice'), ('age', 25), ('city', 'Wonderland'))
data_dict = dict(data_tuples)
print(data_dict)
# Outputs: {'name': 'Alice', 'age': 25, 'city': 'Wonderland'}
```

Using the **dict()** function here simplifies managing the data and allows you to access values using keys, enhancing the flexibility of your code.

Lastly, don't forget that certain data types can be complex, and Python provides functions to handle these too. For instance, converting integers to their ASCII character equivalents can be done with the **chr()** function:

```python
ascii_value = 65
char = chr(ascii_value)
print(char)  # Outputs: A
```

Applied Variable Manipulation

Wizards in Pythonia have the power to shape outcomes through variable manipulation. This journey starts by presenting scenarios that require the initial assignment of variable values. Let's consider a simple task: calculating the total cost of a shopping list. You need to assign initial values to variables that represent the prices of items.

```
apple_price = 0.50
banana_price = 0.30
orange_price = 0.80
```

Here, we've assigned float values to the variables **apple_price**, **banana_price**, and **orange_price**. Each value represents the cost of an individual item. Next, we'll perform various calculations using these assigned variables to find out how much it costs to buy a certain number of apples, bananas, and oranges.

Suppose you want to buy 10 apples, 5 bananas, and 8 oranges:

```
total_cost = (10 * apple_price) + (5 * banana_price) + (8 * orange_price)
print("The total cost is:", total_cost)
```

Breaking this down, each line multiplies the quantity of items by their respective prices and adds them together to get **total_cost**. Here, multiplication and addition of variables show how simple arithmetic operations can be performed using assigned variables. Your **output** should be *The total cost is: 12.9.*

Now, let's shift our focus to manipulating string data. Suppose you're creating a user profile for a new online platform. You'll need to combine first and last names into a single string to display the full name.

```
first_name = "John"
last_name = "Doe"
full_name = first_name + " " + last_name
print("Full Name:", full_name)
```

By using the + operator, we concatenate **first_name** and **last_name** with a space in between to generate the **full_name**.

Moving forward, let's integrate different data types and operations to solve a more complex problem. These in Pythonia are known as the Variable Vortex. Here's how to handle them, just in case.

Right now, you need to process and format user input to create a summary report. Here's an example:

```python
# User inputs
name = "Alice"
age = 30
hours_worked = 45.75
hourly_rate = 20.0

# Calculations
total_earnings = hours_worked * hourly_rate

# String Manipulation
report = f"Employee Name: {name}\nAge: {age}\nTotal Earnings:
${total_earnings:.2f}"
print(report)
```

In this scenario, we see multiple data types being used: strings for **name**, integers for **age**, and floats for **hours_worked** and **hourly_rate**. The calculation involves multiplying hours worked by the hourly rate to find **total_earnings**. We then use an f-string to format and compile all this information into a readable report format. This final formatted string includes all the necessary details, ensuring clarity and precision.

To master these skills, it's crucial to practice integrating data types and operations to achieve specific results. Exercises can range from solving real-world problems like budgeting or creating data summaries to fun puzzles such as generating random passwords based on user input.

For instance, creating a simple budget calculator might involve assigning and calculating various expenses and incomes:

```python
# Initial assignments
income = 3000.00
rent = 800.00
utilities = 150.00
groceries = 200.00

# Calculations
total_expenses = rent + utilities + groceries
savings = income - total_expenses

# Output
```

```
print(f"Total Expenses: ${total_expenses:.2f}")
print(f"Savings: ${savings:.2f}")
```

This script assigns values to various expense categories, calculates the total expenses, and then determines the remaining savings. In this case, the *.2f* format specifier is used in programming to format a floating-point number to two decimal places. This kind of practical application helps embed an understanding of variable manipulation and arithmetic operations.

Final Boss: The Return of the Variable Vortex

Right now, you're prepared to continue with your adventure through Pythonia, while suddenly you see a very rare riddle in the sky. Is that... a Variable Vortex? You learned about it, so it can't be that difficult, right?

You take a look at the riddle and see that the goal is to solve it by using variable manipulation. The riddle states: "You have three containers: 1 holding 12 liters of water, another holding 7 liters of water, and a 3rd one that's empty but can hold up to 15 liters. Transfer the water so that each container ends up with an equal amount."

Let's resolve it! Using code, you could approach the solution as follows:

```
container1 = 12
container2 = 7
container3 = 0

# Equal distribution formula
total_water = container1 + container2 + container3
equal_amount = total_water / 3

# Adjusting the containers
container1 = equal_amount
container2 = equal_amount
container3 = equal_amount

# Output
print(f"Container 1: {container1} liters")
print(f"Container 2: {container2} liters")
print(f"Container 3: {container3} liters")
```

If you sum the total amount of water and then divide it equally among the three containers, this script efficiently solves the problem.

Phew, that was close, now you can continue with your adventure. See? It might seem difficult, but we are all capable of handling everything.

As you continue, remember that mastering variables and data types is a crucial step toward becoming proficient in Python. With type conversion, you now know how to change data from one form to another, enhancing both flexibility and functionality in your scripts. Now, let's continue with our adventure!

CHAPTER 2

Loops Lagoon

Welcome to Loops Lagoon, your next stop in Pythonia. Here, Py awaits, ready to guide you through the incredible world of loops and conditionals. These seemingly simple structures are the backbone of efficient and powerful code writing. But before you can fully explore, you must cross a long lake.

for Loops

As you face the complex waterways of programming, one of your most reliable tools is the **for** loop. This loop helps you navigate through sequences with precision and efficiency, allowing you to automate repetitive tasks, making your code more efficient and reducing human error.

Iteration in programming is like rowing through each section of a river—you repeat certain actions for every "item" in a sequence, ensuring none are left behind. This method is crucial for automating tasks, saving time, enhancing readability, and leveraging computational power to handle large datasets or process numerous actions quickly.

Let's break down **for** loops using practical examples. Remember the wizard's list of fruits in the Valley of Variables? Suppose we want to print each fruit's name:

```python
fruits = ["apple", "banana", "cherry"]
for fruit in fruits:
    print(fruit)
```

In this example, **fruit** takes the value of each item in the list **fruits**. The loop starts with "apple" and prints it, then moves to "banana" and finally "cherry." This simple but powerful mechanism ensures each item in the list is processed.

for loops aren't limited to lists; they work equally well with strings. Think of a string as a collection of characters. If you have the string **message = "hello"**, and you want to print each character separately, you can use:

```
message = "hello"
for char in message:
    print(char)
```

The loop iterates over each character, printing them one by one. This versatility in handling different data types makes **for** loops indispensable.

Real-world applications of **for** loops are many. They're used for data analysis, where you might need to process large datasets row by row. In web development, you could iterate over elements on a webpage to apply styles or gather data. Game developers use them to update game states or generate levels, ensuring each element of their game world is attended to in turn.

To write efficient and readable **for** loops, follow these best practices:

1. **Keep it simple:** Aim for clarity over complexity. A loop should be easy to understand at a glance. Naming variables intuitively helps, like using **fruit** for items in a fruit list, rather than generic terms like **i**.

2. **Limit scope:** Only include essential code within the loop to avoid unnecessary computations. For instance, calculations or function calls that don't change with each iteration should be placed outside the loop.

3. **Use built-in functions:** Python offers several functions that can simplify loop operations, like **enumerate()** for getting an index along with the item, or **zip()** for iterating over multiple sequences simultaneously.

4. **Avoid hard coding:** Instead of hardcoding values, make your loops dynamic. For example, using **len()** to determine the bounds helps adapt your code to different dataset sizes seamlessly.

5. **Break and continue wisely:** While primarily used in other subpoints, knowing when and how to exit or skip parts of a loop can enhance performance and readability.

while Loops

while loops are a foundational concept in programming that allows for the execution of a set of instructions repeatedly based on a given condition. Understanding their mechanics and use cases will enable you to handle repetitive tasks more efficiently.

At its core, a **while** loop executes a block of code as long as a specified condition remains true. The structure is straightforward: It begins with the **while** keyword followed by a condition. If this condition evaluates to true, the loop continues; if false, the loop terminates. Here's a simple example in Python:

```
count = 0
while count < 5:
    print("Count:", count)
    count += 1
```

In this snippet, the loop will execute until **count** reaches 5. Each iteration prints the current value of **count** and increments it by one.

Condition checking is crucial in **while** loops. Before each iteration, the loop evaluates whether the condition is still true. This check determines if the loop should proceed or halt. For instance, in the example above, **while count < 5** is the condition. As long as **count** is less than 5, the loop runs. When **count** becomes 5, the condition fails, and the loop exits.

One common pitfall with **while** loops is the risk of creating an infinite loop, where the condition never evaluates to false, causing the loop to run indefinitely. Consider the following faulty loop:

```
count = 0
while count < 5:
    print("This will print forever!")
```

Since there's no code updating **count**, the condition **count < 5** always holds true, and the loop never stops. To avoid such issues, it's vital to update control variables within the loop body appropriately.

Here's how you could modify the previous example to ensure the loop terminates:

```
count = 0
while count < 5:
    print("Count:", count)
    count += 1  # Updating the control variable
```

By incrementing **count** inside the loop, we ensure the condition will eventually fail, preventing an infinite loop.

while loops are particularly useful when the number of iterations is not predetermined. Let's explore some practical scenarios where **while** loops shine.

User Input Validation

When dealing with user input, ensuring valid entries is critical. Imagine a program that prompts users for a positive integer. You can employ a **while** loop to keep asking for input until a valid response is received:

```
user_input = -1
while user_input <= 0:
    user_input = int(input("Enter a positive number: "))
    if user_input <= 0:
        print("That's not a positive number! Try again.")
```

Here, the loop continuously requests input until the condition **user_input > 0** is met, ensuring the program only proceeds with a valid positive integer.

Searching Through Data

while loops are excellent for searching operations where the number of elements to search through isn't known upfront. For example, in a binary search algorithm used to find a specific element in a sorted list, a **while** loop can efficiently narrow down the search range:

```
def binary_search(arr, target):
    left, right = 0, len(arr) - 1
    while left <= right:
        mid = (left + right) // 2
        if arr[mid] == target:
            return mid
        elif arr[mid] < target:
            left = mid + 1
        else:
```

```
        right = mid - 1
    return -1
```

The loop continues to divide the search range until the target is found or the range is exhausted.

Game Loops

Games often rely on **while** loops to maintain continuous gameplay until a certain condition, like the player losing or winning, is met. Here's a simplified game loop:

```
game_over = False
while not game_over:
    # Game logic
    user_action = input("Continue playing? (yes/no): ")
    if user_action == "no":
        game_over = True
```

In this example, the game keeps running, executing its logic, until the player decides to quit by setting **game_over** to true.

Understanding how to troubleshoot **while** loops is important in becoming a proficient programmer. Infinite loops can occur for various reasons, such as failing to update control variables or misusing logical operators. Here are some troubleshooting techniques:

1. **Proper update of variables:** Always ensure that the variables affecting the loop condition are updated correctly within the loop body. This helps in changing the condition to false eventually.

```python
count = 1
while count <= 5:
print(count)
count += 1  # Properly updating the variable
```

2. **Logical operators:** Be cautious with logical operators in conditions. Misuse can lead to conditions that are always true or false, causing unintended behavior.

```python
count = 1
```

```
while count < 5 and count > 0:    # Correct use of && operator
print(count)
count += 1
```
```

3. **Conditional breakpoints:** Use debugging tools to set breakpoints that activate under specific conditions. This helps pause the execution and examine the state of variables to identify faults.

4. **Step-by-step debugging:** Analyze your code execution step-by-step to understand the flow and identify where the loop might go wrong.

# Loop Control

Right now, you and Py encounter the concepts of **break** and **continue** statements, which are essential tools for managing the flow of loops efficiently.

The **break** statement is used to exit a loop prematurely. Imagine you're in a situation where you're searching for a specific item in a list. Once you find it, there's no need to continue checking the remaining items. Using **break** helps you exit the loop as soon as your condition is met, saving both time and computational resources. For example, consider a loop that checks if a number exists in an array:

```
numbers = [1, 2, 3, 4, 5]
for num in numbers:
    if num == 3:
        print("Found 3!")
        break
```

In this snippet, the loop exits immediately after finding the number 3. Without the **break** statement, the loop would continue to check the remaining numbers unnecessarily.

On the other hand, the **continue** statement allows you to skip the current iteration of the loop and proceed to the next one. This is particularly useful when you need to bypass certain conditions without breaking out of the loop entirely. For instance, imagine a scenario where you want to print only the even numbers from 1 to 10:

```
for i in range(1, 11):
    if i % 2 != 0:
```
```

```
        continue
    print(i)
```

Here, the loop skips all odd numbers thanks to the **continue** statement and prints only the even ones.

Now, let's examine more complex looping scenarios that combine both **break** and **continue** statements. Consider a situation where you need to process a list of integers and stop as soon as you find a negative number, but you also want to skip any zeros within the list:

```
numbers = [2, 0, -1, 5, 0, 3, -4, 8]
for num in numbers:
    if num < 0:
        break
    if num == 0:
        continue
    print(num)
```

In this scenario, the loop will terminate as soon as it encounters the first negative number, -1. It will print all non-zero positive numbers before hitting the **break** statement. Zeroes are skipped because of the **continue** statement.

Understanding how to use **break** and **continue** statements effectively can have a significant impact on the efficiency and readability of your code. Efficient loops ensure that your programs run faster by eliminating unnecessary iterations. In the previous example, the **break** statement prevented additional checks after finding the negative number, which saved processing time.

Furthermore, using **break** and **continue** statements thoughtfully can enhance the readability of your code. These statements make it clear when you want to exit a loop or skip certain iterations based on specific conditions. However, it's important to use these statements sparingly. Overuse can lead to complex, hard-to-follow code structures, similar to the notorious **goto** statements from older programming languages. When used judiciously, **break** and **continue** statements convey intent clearly and help maintain organized, efficient code.

Consider a real-world application such as processing user input in an interactive program. You might want to prompt users to enter their age, but only valid ages (between 0 and 120) should be processed. Invalid input should be skipped, and if users decide to exit by entering a specific value, the loop should terminate:

```
while True:
    age = input("Enter your age (type 'exit' to quit): ")
    if age.lower() == 'exit':
        break
    if not age.isdigit() or not (0 <= int(age) <= 120):
        print("Invalid age. Please try again.")
        continue
    print(f"Your age is: {age}")
```

In this case, the loop continues to prompt the user until they type "exit." Invalid inputs trigger the **continue** statement, directing the loop back to the prompt without processing the input further. Valid ages are printed accordingly.

Efficient loops also contribute to better resource management, especially in larger applications or those running on limited hardware. By exiting loops early or skipping unnecessary iterations, your programs can perform better and avoid potential bottlenecks.

Next, let's consider another practical example involving nested loops. Suppose you're working on a game where you need to check a grid for specific patterns. If you find a match, you might want to break out of the inner loop or even both loops. Here's how you could integrate **break** and **continue** in such a scenario:

```
grid = [
    [0, 1, 2],
    [3, 4, 5],
    [6, 7, 8]
]

for row in grid:
    for col in row:
        if col == 5:
            print("Pattern found at:", col)
            break  # Exit the inner loop
    else:
        continue  # Continue the outer loop if the inner loop wasn't broken
    break  # Break the outer loop if the pattern was found
```

In this example, once the pattern (the number 5) is found, the inner loop breaks, and subsequently, the outer loop also breaks due to the presence of the **break** statement outside the inner loop.

Conditionals

This involves using conditional statements like **if**, **elif**, **else**, and nested conditionals in Python. These tools allow us to specify actions based on certain conditions.

Understanding if Statements

Let's begin with the basic building block: the **if** statement. An **if** statement allows you to execute a block of code only if a specified condition is true. This is incredibly useful for decision-making processes. For example:

```
if 10 > 5:
    print("10 is greater than 5")
print("Program ended")
```

In this example, the condition **10 > 5** evaluates to true, so the program prints, "10 is greater than 5." Regardless of the condition's outcome, the program then prints, "Program ended," demonstrating the flow of control.

Adding Complexity With elif and else

As your decision-making logic grows, you'll need more than just simple **if** statements. This is where **elif** (short for "else if") and else come into play. The **elif** statement allows you to check multiple conditions sequentially, while the **else** statement captures any situations not covered by previous conditions.

Consider the following example:

```
letter = "A"

if letter == "B":
    print("The letter is B")
elif letter == "C":
    print("The letter is C")
elif letter == "A":
    print("The letter is A")
else:
    print("The letter isn't A, B, or C")
```

Here, the code checks if the letter is "B," "C," or "A," and it prints the corresponding message. If none of these conditions are met, the else block executes. This structure is beneficial for handling mutually exclusive scenarios.

Combining Multiple Conditionals

Sometimes you might need to combine conditions to create more complex logical flows. Using logical operators like **and**, **or**, and **not**, you can build more sophisticated conditional statements. For instance:

```python
age = 25
has_license = True


if age >= 18 and has_license:
    print("You can drive.")
else:
    print("You cannot drive.")
```

This example requires both conditions (age being at least 18 and having a license) to be true for the driving permission to be granted. The **and** operator ensures that both conditions must hold.

Nested Conditionals for Harder Decisions

To demonstrate how nested conditionals and loops work together to solve intricate problems, let's consider a scenario where you're managing a list of student grades. You want to categorize these grades into three groups: "Pass," "Merit," and "Distinction." Additionally, any invalid grade (e.g., a negative number or a grade above 100) should be flagged as an error.

Here's how you could approach this:

```python
grades = [85, 42, 90, -3, 76, 105, 67, 88]
for grade in grades:
    if 0 <= grade <= 100:  # Check if the grade is valid
        if grade >= 85:
            print(f"Grade {grade} is a Distinction.")
        elif grade >= 65:
            print(f"Grade {grade} is a Merit.")
        else:
            print(f"Grade {grade} is a Pass.")
    else:
        print(f"Error: Grade {grade} is invalid.")
```

Explanation of the Code

1. **Initial loop:** The **for** loop iterates through each grade in the list **grades**.

2. **First conditional (validity check):** The first **if** statement checks if the grade is valid by ensuring it falls within the range of 0 to 100. If the grade is invalid, the program immediately flags it with an error message.

3. **Nested conditionals:** If the grade is valid, nested conditionals (**if-elif-else**) further classify the grade into one of three categories: "Distinction" (85 and above), "Merit" (65 to 84), and "Pass" (below 65).

4. **Output:** Depending on the condition met, the appropriate message is printed for each grade.

This example showcases how nested conditionals within loops can handle multiple layers of decision-making, ensuring that each grade is not only categorized correctly but also validated for accuracy.

Practical Applications

Nested conditionals within loops are particularly useful in scenarios where you need to handle complex datasets or perform multistep decision-making processes. Examples include

- **Processing data streams:** Continuously evaluate incoming data points, filtering, categorizing, or flagging them based on multiple criteria.

- **Game mechanics:** Manage game states where multiple conditions, such as player actions, game environment, and time limits, must be considered to determine outcomes.

- **Dynamic user interfaces:** Adjust interface elements based on user input and environmental conditions, ensuring that the user interface responds appropriately to a variety of scenarios.

A More Complex Example: Validating and Classifying User Input

Imagine you're building a system that requires users to enter both their age and income level. You want to ensure the age is within a reasonable range and that the income is classified correctly. Here's how you could structure this:

```python
user_data = [
    {'age': 25, 'income': 30000},
    {'age': 17, 'income': 15000},
    {'age': 40, 'income': -20000},
    {'age': 65, 'income': 60000},
    {'age': 30, 'income': 5000},
```

```
]
for data in user_data:
    age = data['age']
    income = data['income']

    if 0 <= age <= 120:  # Valid age check
        if income < 0:
            print(f"Error: Invalid income {income} for age {age}.")
        elif income < 20000:
            print(f"Age {age} with low income ({income})")
        elif income < 50000:
            print(f"Age {age} with medium income ({income})")
        else:
            print(f"Age {age} with high income ({income})")
    else:
        print(f"Error: Invalid age {age}.")
```

Explanation

1. **Looping through data:** The **for** loop iterates through each user's data.

2. **Age validation:** The first **if** checks whether the age is valid. If not, an error message is generated.

3. **Income classification:** If the age is valid, nested conditionals classify the user's income into low, medium, or high categories, or flag it as invalid if it's negative.

See how you can combine loops and nested conditionals to handle difficult tasks? These will ensure your program is both robust and responsive to various input conditions.

Loop Leviathan: The Final Challenge

You've made it through Loops Lagoon! But now, you face the ultimate test—confronting the Loop Leviathan. This fearsome creature challenges you to use everything you've learned to navigate through a maze of tasks. Your goal is to write a script that processes a list of tasks, making decisions at every turn to reach the exit of the maze.

The Maze of Tasks

Imagine you are given a list of tasks representing a maze. Each task can either move you forward, turn you left or right, or indicate an obstacle that you must avoid. Your script must process each task, and your decisions will determine whether you successfully navigate through the maze or get stuck.

Here's a conceptual breakdown:

- **Task list:** The maze is a list of tasks, each represented as a string, like "move forward," "turn left," "turn right," or "obstacle."

- **Goal:** Process the list of tasks using loops and conditionals, navigating through the maze without hitting any obstacles. If an obstacle is encountered, the script should stop and print a message indicating that the path is blocked.

The Script

Let's develop the script step by step:

```python
# Define the list of tasks representing the maze
tasks = ["move forward", "move forward", "turn left", "move forward", "obstacle",
"turn right", "move forward"]

# Initialize variables to keep track of position and direction
position = 0
direction = "north"

# Start navigating through the maze
for task in tasks:
    if task == "move forward":
        position += 1
        print(f"Moved forward to position {position} while facing {direction}.")
    elif task == "turn left":
        if direction == "north":
            direction = "west"
        elif direction == "west":
            direction = "south"
        elif direction == "south":
            direction = "east"
        elif direction == "east":
            direction = "north"
        print(f"Turned left, now facing {direction}.")
    elif task == "turn right":
        if direction == "north":
            direction = "east"
        elif direction == "east":
            direction = "south"
        elif direction == "south":
            direction = "west"
```

```
        elif direction == "west":
            direction = "north"
        print(f"Turned right, now facing {direction}.")
    elif task == "obstacle":
        print(f"Encountered an obstacle at position {position}, cannot proceed.")
        break
    else:
        print(f"Unknown task '{task}' encountered.")

# Check if the maze was completed
if task != "obstacle":
  print(f"Congratulations! You have successfully navigated through the maze and
defeated the Loop Leviathan!")
```

Script Explanation

- **Initialization:** The script starts by initializing the position and direction. The position tracks how far you've moved, and the direction keeps track of which way you're facing.

- **Loop through tasks:** The script iterates through each task in the list using a **for** loop.

- **Conditionals:** Inside the loop, the script uses conditionals (**if, elif, else**) to determine what action to take based on the current task. If the task is "move forward," the script increments the position. If the task is "turn left" or "turn right," the script updates the direction accordingly. If the task is "obstacle," the script stops execution with a **break** statement and prints a message.

- **Completion check:** After processing all tasks, the script checks if the maze was successfully navigated by ensuring no obstacles were encountered.

If your script successfully processes the task list and reaches the end without encountering an obstacle, you've conquered the Loop Leviathan! This challenge not only reinforces your understanding of loops and conditionals but also demonstrates how these concepts work together to solve complex problems.

CHAPTER 3

The Array Archipelago

After successfully navigating the treacherous waters of Loops Lagoon and emerging victorious against the Loop Leviathan, you now set sail toward the heart of the Array Archipelago. This journey is not for the faint-hearted. The archipelago is a complex network of islands, each representing a different data structure in Python—lists, tuples, and sets. At the center of this archipelago lies the most formidable challenge yet: the Array Hydra. To defeat this beast, you must master the powers of these structures, organizing and manipulating data to solve complex problems.

Understanding Lists in Python

Your first stop in the archipelago is the Island of Lists. Lists are your initial weapon against the Array Hydra. They are ordered collections of items, easily modified and expanded. Think of them as your inventory bag, capable of holding anything you collect on your journey—numbers, strings, or even other lists. Creating a list in Python is as simple as writing a set of elements within square brackets [], each item separated by commas. For example:

```python
my_list = [1, 'apple', 3.14, True]
print(my_list)
```

This produces the output:

```
[1, 'apple', 3.14, True]
```

Here, **my_list** contains an integer, a string, a floating-point number, and a Boolean value, illustrating how diverse items can coexist within a single list.

Indexing: Accessing Elements by Position

To confront the Array Hydra, you must master the art of accessing and managing the items on your list. Python uses zero-based indexing, where the first element has an index of 0. This allows you to precisely retrieve and manipulate individual elements:

```
fruits = ['apple', 'banana', 'cherry']
print(fruits[1])  # Output: banana
```

But sometimes, you need more than just a single item. You need to slice through your list, extracting specific portions while leaving the rest intact. Slicing allows you to create new lists from subsets of the original, enabling you to focus on what matters most:

```
numbers = [0, 1, 2, 3, 4, 5, 6]
subset = numbers[2:5]
print(subset)  # Output: [2, 3, 4]
```

Common List Methods

Python provides several built-in methods to manipulate lists dynamically:

•   **append()**: Adds an element to the end of the list.

```
animals = ['cat', 'dog']
animals.append('rabbit')
print(animals)  # Output: ['cat', 'dog', 'rabbit']
```

•   **remove()**: Removes the first occurrence of a specified element.

```
animals.remove('dog')
print(animals)  # Output: ['cat', 'rabbit']
```

- sort(): Sorts the list in ascending order by default.

```
numbers = [3, 1, 4, 1, 5]
numbers.sort()
print(numbers)  # Output: [1, 1, 3, 4, 5]
```

These methods allow you to alter and organize your lists as needed. The **append()** method facilitates the easy addition of new elements, while **remove()** helps maintain clean data sets by eliminating unwanted items. The **sort()** method ensures your list is organized, which can be particularly beneficial when dealing with numerical data or alphabetized lists.

Exploring Tuples as Immutable Sequences

As you sail further, you reach the Immutable Island of Tuples. Tuples are like ancient relics—once created, they cannot be altered. This immutability provides stability, ensuring that data remains consistent and unchanging, even in the face of the Array Hydra's attacks.

Tuples are defined by parentheses and store fixed collections of items:

```
coordinates = (10, 20)
print(coordinates)  # Output: (10, 20)
```

In your adventure, tuples are invaluable for scenarios where data integrity is paramount. For example, returning multiple values from a function as a tuple ensures that the data remains intact during further processing. Another common use case is storing configuration settings or coordinates that should not be modified after being set.

Consider this scenario:

```
settings = ('high', 'medium', 'low')
print(settings)  # Output: ('high', 'medium', 'low')
```

In this case, the tuple ensures that the settings remain consistent, providing a reliable reference point throughout your program.

Mastering Sets: The Island of Uniqueness

Your journey continues to the Island of Sets, where every inhabitant is unique. Sets are unordered collections that do not allow duplicates, making them perfect for managing unique elements. This island is a fortress against redundancy, offering powerful operations to merge, intersect, and differentiate between data.

For example, if you have two sets of favorite fruits:

```python
friend1_fruits = {"apple", "banana", "orange"}
friend2_fruits = {"banana", "kiwi", "grape"}
```

You can find common fruits (intersection) or combine all unique fruits (union):

```python
common_fruits = friend1_fruits & friend2_fruits  # Output: {"banana"}
all_fruits = friend1_fruits | friend2_fruits  # Output: {"apple", "banana",
"orange", "kiwi", "grape"}
```

Sets are your shield against the Hydra's attempts to overwhelm you with duplicates. They are particularly useful for membership testing and ensuring the uniqueness of elements in large datasets.

Confronting the Array Hydra

Finally, the moment has come to face the Array Hydra. This beast is a manifestation of complex data problems that require you to use all the tools at your disposal—sorting, filtering, and combining data across multiple structures.

The Challenge: Sorting and Filtering Data

The Array Hydra will throw a list of tasks at you, each one more complex than the last. You must sort these tasks, filter out the irrelevant ones, and combine elements from different lists to form a coherent strategy.

For example, imagine you have a list of student names and grades:

```python
students = [('Alice', 85), ('Bob', 70), ('Charlie', 95)]
```

You need to sort this list by grades and filter out students who scored below 80:

```
sorted_students = sorted([student for student in students if student[1] > 80],
key=lambda x: x[1])
print(sorted_students)  # Output: [('Alice', 85), ('Charlie', 95)]
```

By mastering these operations, you can quickly identify the top performers while discarding irrelevant data.

The Final Battle: Organizing and Combining Data Structures

To defeat the Hydra, you must combine the strengths of lists, tuples, and sets. Imagine you are managing a project team with a list of members, immutable milestones, and a set of required skills:

```
team_members = ['Alice', 'Bob', 'Charlie']
project_milestones = ('Planning', 'Execution', 'Closure')
required_skills = {'Python', 'Data Analysis', 'Communication'
```

You can dynamically add new members, maintain the integrity of milestones, and ensure skills are unique:

```
team_members.append('Dana')
unique_skills = set(required_skills)
```

By integrating these data structures, you can effectively manage your resources and overcome the Hydra's challenges.

The Final Strike: Combining Operations

The Array Hydra's last stand is a complex problem requiring you to sort, filter, and combine data. For example, managing product sales data:

```
products = [('Laptop', 150), ('Phone', 200), ('Tablet', 50), ('Monitor', 120)]
top_products = sorted([product for product in products if product[1] > 100],
key=lambda x: x[1], reverse=True)

categories = {'Electronics', 'Gadgets', 'Accessories'}
new_categories = {'Wearables', 'Home Appliances'}
all_categories = categories.union(new_categories)

print(top_products)  # Output: [('Phone', 200), ('Laptop', 150), ('Monitor', 120)]
print(all_categories)  # Output: {'Electronics', 'Gadgets', 'Accessories',
'Wearables', 'Home Appliances'}
```

This final combination of operations delivers the decisive blow to the Array Hydra, showcasing your mastery of Python's data structures.

You've emerged victorious against the Array Hydra. Your journey through the Array Archipelago has not only sharpened your skills in organizing and manipulating data but also equipped you with the tools to tackle any data-related challenge Python might throw at you. As you sail away from the archipelago, the conquered Hydra behind you, you know that you're ready for whatever lies ahead in the vast, uncharted waters of programming.

As you continue your adventure, take time to experiment with combining these data structures in your projects. Try creating a simple inventory management system or a basic contact list application using lists, tuples, and sets. The more you practice, the more confident you'll become in wielding these powerful tools.

CHAPTER 4

The Dictionary Desert

After traversing the treacherous waters of Loops Lagoon and defeating the Loop Leviathan, you find yourself amid a vast, arid expanse known as the Dictionary Desert. Here, managing data efficiently is crucial for survival. The heat is relentless, and the dunes stretch endlessly into the horizon, but somewhere within this desert lies the power to control and manipulate vast amounts of information. This power is embodied in the form of Python dictionaries—a tool that allows you to store, retrieve, and organize data with unparalleled precision.

As you venture into the Dictionary Desert, you encounter the ancient secrets of Python dictionaries, also known as hash maps or associative arrays in other programming languages. These collections of key-value pairs are the lifeblood of any seasoned programmer, offering rapid lookups, easy modifications, and the kind of efficiency that can make the difference between life and death in the harsh desert environment.

Dictionaries: Your Compass in the Desert

Dictionaries in Python are like ancient scrolls, filled with key-value pairs where each key acts as a unique identifier that maps directly to a specific value. This uniqueness ensures that each piece of data is easily accessible, saving you from the daunting task of sifting through endless arrays or lists.

Your first lesson in this desert is the importance of choosing meaningful keys. Imagine trying to navigate using a map where the landmarks are labeled with random numbers rather than descriptive names. It would be nearly impossible to find your way. Similarly, when creating dictionaries, using keys like **'title'**, **'author'**, and 'year' not only makes your code efficient but also ensures that anyone—including your future self—can easily understand what each key represents. This practice enhances both the efficiency and readability of your code, much like a well-drawn map in the desert sands.

Creating a dictionary in Python is akin to drawing your first map in the desert. There are two primary methods: using curly braces and the **dict()** function. Here's how you can create a dictionary using curly braces:

```python
# Using curly braces
book_details = {
    "title": "1984",
    "author": "George Orwell",
    "year": 1949
}
```

In this example, the keys are 'title', 'author', and 'year', each mapping to relevant values about the book *1984*. Alternatively, you can use the **dict()** function to achieve the same result:

```python
# Using the dict() function
book_details = dict(title="1984", author="George Orwell", year=1949)
```

Both methods yield the same structure, allowing flexibility based on your coding style or requirements. With your first map in hand, you can now navigate the Dictionary Desert with more confidence.

Navigating the Dunes: Accessing and Modifying Data

Now that you have your map, it's time to learn how to read it. Accessing values in a dictionary is straightforward—just use the keys to retrieve their corresponding values. Suppose you want to find the author of the book from our **book_details** dictionary:

```python
author = book_details["author"]
print(author)  # Output: George Orwell
```

But beware—the desert is full of hidden traps. If you attempt to access a key that doesn't exist in the dictionary, Python will raise a **KeyError**, much like stumbling into quicksand. To avoid such errors, you can use the **get()** method, which provides a safe route by returning a default value if the key isn't found:

```
publication_year = book_details.get("year", "Not Available")
print(publication_year)  # Output: 1949
```

This approach gives you more control over error handling, ensuring your journey through the desert is as smooth as possible.

As you progress, you'll encounter scenarios where you need to update your map—modifying or adding new key-value pairs to your dictionary. For example, if you discover that the publication year of *1984* needs to be updated:

```
book_details["year"] = 1950
print(book_details["year"])  # Output: 1950
```

Adding new books to your library is equally straightforward:

```
library = {}
library["Brave New World"] = {"author": "Aldous Huxley", "year": 1932, "genre":
"Science Fiction"}
print(library["Brave New World"])
# Output: {'author': 'Aldous Huxley', 'year': 1932, 'genre': 'Science Fiction'}
```

Your ability to manage and update this map will be crucial as you face the more complex territories of the Dictionary Desert.

Complex Data Structures: The Oasis of Nested Dictionaries

After traversing the initial dunes, you stumble upon an oasis—a place where the sands give way to lush greenery and water. Here, you discover the power of nested dictionaries, which allow you to represent complex data hierarchies. These are not just simple maps but multilayered charts that can guide you through the most difficult mazes of data.

Imagine needing to manage information about various employees within a company. A single-level dictionary might suffice for basic attributes, but what if each employee has multiple roles, projects, and performance metrics? This is where nested dictionaries come into play. With a dictionary of dictionaries, each employee can have a unique key that maps to another dictionary containing numerous key-value pairs representing detailed attributes.

For instance:

```python
employees = {
    'Katie': {'Age': 30, 'Job': 'Engineer', 'Projects': ['Project1', 'Project2']},
    'Bryan': {'Age': 25, 'Job': 'Designer', 'Projects': ['Project3']}
}
```

In this example, **employees** is a dictionary where each key (e.g., **'Alice'**) maps to another dictionary containing further details about that employee. This structure allows you to store and retrieve complex information with ease.

As you explore the oasis, you realize that nested dictionaries can simulate a simple database. For instance, a student database might look like this:

```python
students = {
    'Student1': {'Name': 'Annie Johnson', 'Age': 20, 'Grades': {'Math': 'A',
'Science': 'B'}},
    'Student2': {'Name': 'Carlos Lopez', 'Age': 22, 'Grades': {'Math': 'B',
'Science': 'A'}}
}
```

Here, each student identifier maps to a dictionary containing personal details and another nested dictionary for grades, closely resembling a relational database table.

Accessing these nested structures is as straightforward as following a well-marked path through the oasis. To retrieve John's age from the aforementioned student database:

```python
age_of_john = students['Student1']['Age']
```

Updating values is just as simple:

```python
students['Student2']['Grades']['Math'] = 'A+'
```

These examples show how nested dictionaries can turn complex data into manageable structures, much like turning a barren desert into a thriving oasis.

However, every oasis has its dangers. The deeper you delve into nested dictionaries, the more complex they become, and the more likely you are to encounter challenges. Accessing and modifying deeply nested values can lead to verbose code and potential errors if keys are missing or misspelled. Moreover, deeply nested structures can become difficult to comprehend and maintain, obscuring the overall data architecture.

Despite these challenges, the benefits often outweigh the risks. Nested dictionaries allow for highly organized and modular data storage, making them adept at handling complex datasets where relationships between data points must be preserved. They facilitate efficient querying and manipulation, crucial for applications requiring rapid data access and updates.

An essential technique in managing this complexity is the use of dictionary methods, which simplify interactions with these nested structures. For instance, the **get**() method helps to safely retrieve values without raising errors if a key doesn't exist:

```
math_grade = students['Student2'].get('Grades', {}).get('Math', 'No grade
available')
```

This method elegantly handles cases where a key might be absent, returning a default message instead of causing a program crash.

As you explore further, you find that iterating over these nested structures can reveal new insights, much like discovering hidden springs in the oasis. Whether it's keys, values, or entire key-value pairs, iteration facilitates comprehensive data analysis and modification. For example, if you want to list all students' names along with their science grades:

```
for student, details in students.items():
    print(f"{details['Name']} - Science Grade: {details['Grades'].get('Science',
'Not enrolled')}")
```

This loop traverses the **students** dictionary, extracts necessary details, and formats them for readability.

The Journey Through the Desert: Iterating Over Dictionaries

Leaving the oasis behind, you continue your journey through the Dictionary Desert, armed with the knowledge of nested dictionaries. The next challenge you face is learning how to efficiently traverse and manipulate the data within your dictionaries. Iterating over dictionaries is like exploring every nook and cranny of the desert, ensuring no detail is overlooked.

Iterating Over Keys Using a for Loop

A fundamental way to iterate through a dictionary is by using a for loop to traverse its keys. Each key in the dictionary can be accessed and processed individually:

```python
data = {'name': 'Marie', 'age': 25, 'city': 'Kansas'}
for key in data:
    print(f"Key: {key}")
```

In this snippet, the loop goes through each key and prints it out. This approach is particularly useful when you only need to work with the keys without immediately requiring their associated values.

Iterating Over Values Using the values() Method

Sometimes, you might want to focus solely on the values within a dictionary. The **values()** method provides a straightforward way to achieve this:

```python
for value in data.values():
    print(f"Value: {value}")
```

Here, the loop iterates through the values returned by the **values()** method, allowing you to process them independently from their keys. This method is beneficial when the values are the primary focus of your task.

Iterating Over Key-Value Pairs Using the items() Method

One of the most versatile ways to iterate over a dictionary is by using the **items()** method, which allows you to access both keys and values simultaneously. This method can be particularly powerful for tasks that require processing and utilizing both elements:

```python
for key, value in data.items():
    print(f"Key: {key}, Value: {value}")
```

By unpacking the items returned by the **items()** method, you get direct access to each key-value pair, making your iteration more intuitive and effective.

Practical Applications of Iterating

Understanding how to iterate through dictionaries is not just about knowing the syntax. It has significant real-world implications, especially for tasks like data filtering and aggregation.

Data Filtering

Imagine you have a dictionary containing user information, and you want to filter out users based on specific criteria such as age:

```python
users = {
    'user1': {'name': 'Marie', 'age': 25},
    'user2': {'name': 'George', 'age': 30},
    'user3': {'name': 'Charles', 'age': 22}
}

filtered_users = {k: v for k, v in users.items() if v['age'] > 23}
print(filtered_users)
```

In this example, the comprehension filters out any users younger than 24 years old. Iterating through the dictionary with **items()** makes it easy to apply such conditions and extract the relevant data.

Data Aggregation

Aggregating data from a dictionary is another common use case. For instance, suppose you want to calculate the average age of users:

```python
total_age = sum(user['age'] for user in users.values())
average_age = total_age / len(users)
print(f"Average Age: {average_age}")
```

With this, you can quickly sum up ages and then divide by the number of users to find the average. This kind of aggregation is essential in scenarios involving statistical analysis or summary reports.

The Final Boss: Confronting the Key-Guardian

As you near the heart of the Dictionary Desert, you sense a powerful presence looming ahead. The sand shifts under your feet, and a towering figure emerges—the Key-Guardian. This ancient sentinel protects the secrets of the desert, and only those who can wield the power of Python dictionaries with skill and precision can hope to defeat it.

The Key-Guardian is a formidable foe, representing the ultimate challenge in managing and retrieving data. To overcome this guardian, you must develop a script that utilizes dictionaries to manage and retrieve data—essentially creating a simple database query system.

Building the Key-Guardian Script: A Simple Database Query System

To defeat the Key-Guardian, you'll need to demonstrate your mastery of dictionaries by creating a script that can add, search, update, and display data much like a basic database query system.

Step 1: Adding Data to the Dictionary

First, we'll define a function to add new entries to our dictionary:

```python
def add_contact(contacts, name, phone, email):
    contacts[name] = {'phone': phone, 'email': email}
```

This function allows you to add a new contact to your dictionary, which will be your database.

Step 2: Searching for Data

Next, create a function to search for a specific contact:

```python
def search_contact(contacts, name):
    return contacts.get(name, 'Contact not found')
```

This function searches for a contact by name and returns the contact details or a message if the contact is not found.

Step 3: Updating Data

To update existing data, define another function:

```python
def update_contact(contacts, name, phone=None, email=None):
    if name in contacts:
        if phone:
            contacts[name]['phone'] = phone
        if email:
            contacts[name]['email'] = email
    else:
        return 'Contact not found'
```

This function allows you to update the phone number, email, or both for a specific contact.

Step 4: Removing Data

You can also remove a contact using the following function:

```
def remove_contact(contacts, name):
    if name in contacts:
        del contacts[name]
    else:
        return 'Contact not found'
```

This function deletes the contact if it exists in the dictionary.

Step 5: Displaying All Data

Finally, here's a function to display all contacts in the dictionary:

```
def display_contacts(contacts):
    for name, details in contacts.items():
        print(f'Name: {name}, Phone: {details["phone"]}, Email:
{details["email"]}')
```

This function iterates over the dictionary and prints out each contact's details.

Step 6: Bringing It All Together

With all the components in place, you can now implement the Key-Guardian script:

```
if __name__ == "__main__":
    contacts = {}
    add_contact(contacts, 'Marie Lou', '555-555-1111', 'marie.lou@example.com')
    add_contact(contacts, 'Bryan Luke', '555-555-2222', 'bryan.luke@example.com')

    print(search_contact(contacts, 'Marie Lou'))

    update_contact(contacts, 'Marie Lou', email='marie.lou@example.com')
    display_contacts(contacts)

    remove_contact(contacts, 'Bryan Luke')
    display_contacts(contacts)
```

This script allows you to manage and retrieve data efficiently, resembling a basic database query system. If you demonstrate your ability to control the flow of information through the Dictionary Desert, you ultimately defeat the Key-Guardian.

Congrats! With the Key-Guardian vanquished, you emerge from the Dictionary Desert as a master of data management. You've learned how to create, access, and modify dictionaries, explore the complexities of nested dictionaries, and efficiently iterate over dictionary elements. Your journey has equipped you with the skills to build robust and maintainable applications that handle structured data with ease and precision.

As you leave the desert behind, the tools and knowledge you've acquired will serve you well in the many challenges that lie ahead. Whether you're managing a simple contact list or developing a complex data system, you now possess the key to unlock the full potential of Python dictionaries—one of the most powerful weapons in your programming arsenal.

CHAPTER 5

The OOP Labyrinth

As the mist clears and you step into the OOP Labyrinth, you find yourself at the entrance of a confusing maze. The air is thick with the promise of discovery, and every twist and turn of the labyrinth seems to pulse with the energy of object-oriented programming (OOP). This is no ordinary journey; it is a quest to master the principles that will allow you to build elegant, efficient, and scalable software. Each path you take will lead you deeper into the heart of OOP, where the final challenge awaits: the legendary Class Chimera.

In this journey, you will explore the essential concepts of classes and objects, inheritance, encapsulation, and polymorphism. These principles are not just abstract ideas—they are the tools and weapons you will wield to conquer the labyrinth and emerge as a true master of OOP. But beware, for the labyrinth is filled with trials that will test your understanding and push your skills to their limits.

The Gateway to the Labyrinth: Understanding Classes and Objects

Your first steps into the labyrinth bring you face-to-face with its gateway—classes and objects. These are the fundamental building blocks of OOP, the very foundation upon which the entire labyrinth is constructed.

A class is a detailed plan that outlines the attributes and behaviors of the entities you will encounter. Imagine it as the architectural design of a grand castle, detailing every room, hallway, and tower. A class defines what properties (attributes) an object will have and what actions (methods) it can perform. For example, in your quest, you might define a **Knight** class, which includes attributes such as armor, weapon, and strength, and methods like **attack()** and **defend()**.

Creating an object from a class is like bringing this blueprint to life. When you instantiate a class, you create an object—a specific instance of that class, complete with its own set of attributes and behaviors. This is akin to constructing a castle from its blueprint, bringing stone and mortar together to create a physical structure. For example, by instantiating the **Knight** class, you might create a character named Sir Lancelot, clad in gleaming armor and armed with a sharp sword.

Let's walk through the creation of a simple **Knight** class:

```python
class Knight:
    def __init__(self, name, armor, weapon, strength):
        self.name = name
        self.armor = armor
        self.weapon = weapon
        self.strength = strength

    def attack(self):
        return f"{self.name} attacks with {self.weapon}, dealing {self.strength} damage!"

    def defend(self):
        return f"{self.name} defends with {self.armor}, reducing damage by half!"
```

With this class defined, you can create an object—your knight—ready to embark on quests within the labyrinth:

```python
sir_lancelot = Knight("Sir Lancelot", "Steel Armor", "Sword", 50)
print(sir_lancelot.attack())
print(sir_lancelot.defend())
```

In this example, Sir Lancelot is an object with attributes like **name**, **armor**, **weapon**, and **strength**. The **attack()** and **defend()** methods allow him to interact with the world around him, striking down enemies and blocking incoming attacks.

As you progress through the labyrinth, you will encounter many more opportunities to create and use classes and objects. Each class you define is like a new weapon or tool in your arsenal, and each object you create is a character or item that will help you navigate the challenges ahead.

But the labyrinth is vast, and Sir Lancelot's journey has only just begun. To truly master the labyrinth, you must explore the pathways of inheritance, encapsulation, and polymorphism—the advanced concepts that will allow you to build more powerful and flexible systems.

The Hidden Passageways: Exploring Inheritance

As you venture deeper into the labyrinth, you discover a hidden passageway that leads to the concept of **inheritance**. This powerful tool allows you to build upon existing classes, creating new ones that inherit the attributes and methods of their predecessors. It's like discovering that the castle you've built can be expanded into a fortress, with new towers and battlements added to the original structure.

Inheritance is a way to extend and refine your classes, allowing you to create more specialized and complex objects without duplicating code. Imagine that you've already mastered the **Knight** class and now wish to create a more powerful type of knight—a **Paladin**, who possesses both the martial prowess of a knight and the divine powers of a cleric. Instead of starting from scratch, you can inherit the **Knight** class and add new attributes and methods that define the unique abilities of a **Paladin**.

```python
class Paladin(Knight):
    def __init__(self, name, armor, weapon, strength, holy_power):
        super().__init__(name, armor, weapon, strength)
        self.holy_power = holy_power

    def heal(self):
        return f"{self.name} uses holy power to heal for {self.holy_power}
health!"
```

With the **Paladin** class, you can now create a character who not only fights with sword and shield but also calls upon divine powers to heal allies or smite enemies:

```python
sir_galahad = Paladin("Sir Galahad", "Blessed Armor", "Holy Sword", 60, 30)
print(sir_galahad.attack())
print(sir_galahad.heal())
```

Inheritance allows you to extend the functionality of a base class like **Knight** and create new, specialized classes like **Paladin** without duplicating code. This not only saves time but also makes your code more organized and easier to maintain. Each class in your codebase becomes a building block that you can refine and expand, much like how a skilled blacksmith refines each weapon they forge.

Inheritance also enables you to create a hierarchy of classes, where each level of the hierarchy represents a more specialized version of the classes above it. This is like constructing a series of fortifications, each one more advanced and better defended than the last. For example, you could create a **HolyKnight** class that inherits from **Paladin**, adding even more powerful divine abilities:

```
class HolyKnight(Paladin):
    def smite(self, target):
        return f"{self.name} smites {target.name} with divine power, dealing
{self.holy_power + 10} damage!"
```

But beware—inheritance also comes with its challenges. Overrelying on inheritance can lead to tightly coupled code, where changes to a parent class might inadvertently affect its child classes. As you traverse the labyrinth, remember to use inheritance wisely, balancing the benefits of code reuse with the need for flexibility and clarity.

The Labyrinth Walls: Encapsulation in OOP

The walls of the labyrinth are tall and imposing, and as you walk along them, you realize they are not just physical barriers but also metaphors for **encapsulation**—a fundamental principle of OOP that protects the integrity of your code by controlling access to an object's data.

Encapsulation is like the armor of a knight, shielding the most vital parts of an object from external forces. In OOP, encapsulation is achieved by keeping certain attributes and methods private, accessible only within the class itself, while exposing others through public interfaces. This ensures that the internal state of an object can only be changed in controlled ways, preventing unintended interference and maintaining the integrity of your code.

To see encapsulation in action, let's revisit our **Knight** class and modify it to protect its attributes:

```
class Knight:
    def __init__(self, name, armor, weapon, strength):
        self._name = name
        self._armor = armor
```

```python
        self._weapon = weapon
        self._strength = strength

    def attack(self):
        return f"{self._name} attacks with {self._weapon}, dealing {self._strength}
damage!"

    def defend(self):
        return f"{self._name} defends with {self._armor}, reducing damage by
half!"

    def get_name(self):
        return self._name

    def set_name(self, name):
        if name:
            self._name = name
```

In this example, the attributes **name**, **armor**, **weapon**, and **strength** are now private, indicated by the underscore prefix (_). These attributes cannot be accessed directly from outside the class, protecting them from accidental modification. Instead, you provide public methods, like **get_name**() and **set_name**(), to allow controlled access to these attributes.

Encapsulation not only protects your code from errors but also makes it more modular. If you hide the internal details of a class, you can change its implementation without affecting the rest of your program. This is akin to upgrading a knight's armor without altering their combat style—your code remains robust and flexible, able to adapt to new challenges as you delve deeper into the labyrinth.

Moreover, encapsulation plays a crucial role in maintaining the integrity of an object's state. By controlling access to an object's attributes, you prevent external entities from putting the object into an invalid or inconsistent state, thereby making your code more reliable and easier to debug.

Encapsulation also helps to enforce the single-responsibility principle, one of the key tenets of OOP. This principle states that each class should have only one responsibility or reason to change. If you encapsulate the data and methods of a class, you ensure that each class has a clear and focused purpose, making your code easier to understand and maintain.

For example, you might decide to create a separate **Weapon** class that handles all the details of a knight's weapon, such as its type, damage, and durability. By encapsulating this information within the **Weapon** class, you keep the **Knight** class focused on its core responsibilities—fighting and defending—while allowing the **Weapon** class to handle all the details related to weaponry.

```
class Weapon:
    def __init__(self, name, damage, durability):
        self._name = name
        self._damage = damage
        self._durability = durability

    def use(self):
        self._durability -= 1
        return f"{self._name} is used, dealing {self._damage} damage. Durability
is now {self._durability}."
```

Using encapsulation in this way, you create a system that is both flexible and resilient, capable of adapting to new requirements and challenges without breaking.

The Shifting Walls: Harnessing Polymorphism

As you journey further into the labyrinth, the walls begin to shift and change, much like the concept of polymorphism in OOP. Polymorphism allows different objects to respond uniquely to the same method call, depending on their specific implementations. It is the art of creating flexible and adaptable code, much like a master swordsman who can wield any weapon with equal skill.

Polymorphism is one of the most powerful tools in your OOP arsenal, allowing you to write code that can work with objects of different classes through a common interface. This makes your programs more flexible, scalable, and easier to extend.

Consider a scenario where you have a **Knight**, a **Paladin**, and a **Rogue**—each with a different fighting style. With polymorphism, you can create a method that lets any character attack, regardless of their specific class:

```
class Rogue(Knight):
    def attack(self):
        return f"{self._name} strikes swiftly with {self._weapon}, dealing
{self._strength + 10} damage!"

characters = [sir_lancelot, sir_galahad, Rogue("Shadow", "Leather Armor",
"Dagger", 40)]
```

```
for character in characters:
    print(character.attack())
```

In this example, each character's **attack**() method behaves differently, depending on whether the character is a **Knight**, a **Paladin**, or a **Rogue**. Polymorphism allows you to treat different objects in a unified way, enabling them to respond according to their unique behaviors.

Polymorphism also makes it easier to extend your code. For example, if you later decide to add a **Mage** class with its own unique **attack**() method, you can do so without modifying the existing code:

```python
pythonCopy codeclass Mage(Knight):
    def attack(self):
        return f"{self._name} casts a spell, dealing {self._strength + 15} magical
damage!"
```

This enhances your code's flexibility, allowing you to extend and modify your program without rewriting existing code. As you traverse the labyrinth, you'll find that polymorphism is one of your most powerful tools, enabling you to adapt to new challenges and create dynamic, interactive systems.

Polymorphism also exemplifies the principle of loose coupling, where the interactions between components are minimal and well-defined. This principle is crucial for building scalable systems, as it allows you to change or extend parts of the system without impacting the rest of the codebase.

The Final Chamber: Confronting the Class Chimera

At the heart of the labyrinth lies the Class Chimera, a fearsome creature that embodies the complexity and power of OOP. To defeat this mythical beast, you must bring together all the principles you've learned—classes, inheritance, encapsulation, and polymorphism—and construct a complex system that can stand against the Chimera's might.

The Class Chimera is a creature of many forms, able to shift and adapt to any challenge you present. To defeat it, you must create a system that is equally flexible, powerful, and adaptable.

Imagine you're building an RPG game where characters interact dynamically. You'll need to design a system that incorporates multiple classes, each with its own attributes and methods, and allows these characters to engage in quests, navigate dungeons, and battle enemies.

Step 1: Designing the Foundation Classes

Begin by designing foundational classes like **Character**, **Weapon**, and **Armor**. The **Character** class will hold attributes such as **name**, **health**, and **strength**, along with methods like **attack()** and **defend()**. The **Weapon** and **Armor** classes will include attributes pertinent to their functions, such as **damage_points** for weapons and **defense_rating** for armor.

```python
class Character:
    def __init__(self, name, health, strength):
        self._name = name
        self._health = health
        self._strength = strength
        self._inventory = []

    def attack(self, target):
        damage = self._strength
        target._health -= damage
        return f"{self._name} attacks {target._name} for {damage} damage!"

    def defend(self, damage):
        self._health -= damage // 2
        return f"{self._name} defends and takes {damage // 2} damage!"

class Weapon:
    def __init__(self, name, damage_points):
        self._name = name
        self._damage_points = damage_points

class Armor:
    def __init__(self, name, defense_rating):
        self._name = name
        self._defense_rating = defense_rating
```

Step 2: Implementing Inheritance and Polymorphism

Next, create subclasses that inherit from **Character**, such as **Warrior**, **Mage**, and **Rogue**. Each subclass can override the **attack()** method to reflect their unique combat styles, showcasing polymorphism.

```python
class Warrior(Character):
    def attack(self, target):
        damage = self._strength + 5
        target._health -= damage
```

```
            return f"{self._name}, the Warrior, strikes {target._name} with a sword
for {damage} damage!"

class Mage(Character):
    def attack(self, target):
        damage = self._strength + 3
        target._health -= damage
        return f"{self._name}, the Mage, casts a spell on {target._name} for {damage}
damage!"

class Rogue(Character):
    def attack(self, target):
        damage = self._strength + 4
        target._health -= damage
        return f"{self._name}, the Rogue, sneaks behind {target._name} and deals
{damage} damage!"
```

Step 3: Integrating the System

Design other classes like **Dungeon** and **Quest**, each with distinct attributes and methods. Characters can undertake quests, navigate dungeons, and engage in battles, demonstrating the interplay between various classes.

```
class Dungeon:
    def __init__(self, name, difficulty_level, enemies):
        self._name = name
        self._difficulty_level = difficulty_level
        self._enemies = enemies

    def enter(self, character):
        for enemy in self._enemies:
            result = character.attack(enemy)
            print(result)
            if enemy._health <= 0:
                print(f"{enemy._name} is defeated!")

class Quest:
    def __init__(self, name, objective):
        self._name = name
        self._objective = objective

    def start(self, character):
        print(f"{character._name} begins the quest: {self._name}")
```

```python
        print(f"Objective: {self._objective}")
        return f"{character._name} has completed the quest!"
```

Step 4: Confronting the Class Chimera

Now that you've constructed the components, you're ready to confront the Class Chimera. This system simulates an RPG game where characters interact, take on quests, and battle enemies.

```python
if __name__ == "__main__":
    warrior = Warrior("Aragorn", 100, 15)
    mage = Mage("Gandalf", 80, 12)
    rogue = Rogue("Legolas", 90, 14)

    orc = Character("Orc", 50, 10)
    troll = Character("Troll", 70, 12)

    dungeon = Dungeon("Moria", 3, [orc, troll])

    print(dungeon.enter(warrior))
    print(dungeon.enter(mage))
    print(dungeon.enter(rogue))

    quest = Quest("Destroy the One Ring", "Throw the ring into Mount Doom")
    print(quest.start(warrior))
```

In this final battle, you have confronted the Class Chimera and emerged victorious, demonstrating your ability to construct complex systems using OOP principles.

Congratulations! With the Class Chimera defeated, you emerge from the OOP Labyrinth as a master of OOP. You've learned how to create, use, and integrate classes, understand the power of inheritance, encapsulation, and polymorphism, and apply these principles to build complex, interactive systems.

As you leave the labyrinth behind, the skills and knowledge you've gained will serve you well in future challenges. Whether developing a simple application or a large-scale system, you now have the tools to create robust, scalable, and maintainable software. The OOP Labyrinth is a journey you will revisit often, but each time, you will find yourself more capable of facing its twists and turns.

CHAPTER 6

The Debugging Jungle

Facing the world of coding errors is akin to trekking through a dense, unpredictable jungle. Every step forward reveals new challenges: tangled vines of syntax mistakes, hidden pitfalls of logic errors, and the lurking dangers of runtime issues. The path is treacherous, but it's one that every coder must walk to transform from a novice to a proficient programmer. Mastering the art of debugging is not just about fixing errors; it's about understanding your code on a deeper level, ensuring it runs smoothly, and preparing yourself for the ultimate test—the Final Boss: Error Entity.

In this chapter, you'll encounter common syntax errors that halt your progress, like missing colons, unmatched parentheses, and incorrect indentation. As you move, you'll face execution errors—those that occur during runtime—such as division by zero, accessing undefined variables, and using out-of-range indices. Finally, you'll confront the most insidious of all: logical flaws that might not trigger visible crashes but lead to incorrect results.

The Jungle Underbrush: Common Syntax Errors

As you take your first steps into the jungle, you encounter the thick underbrush—syntax errors. These errors are like the vines that can trip you up if you're not careful. Identifying and correcting these common mistakes is crucial for any developer. By understanding how missing colons, unmatched parentheses, and incorrect indentation can lead to these errors, and recognizing the impact of misspelled keywords or variables, you will become adept at navigating this treacherous terrain.

Tangled Vines: Missing Colons and Unmatched Parentheses

One of the most common syntax errors that can halt your progress is a missing colon. In Python, colons indicate the start of an indented block, whether it's for loops, conditional statements, or function definitions. A missing colon is like a missing signpost in the jungle, leaving you lost and confused.

Consider this simple if statement:

```
if True
    print("This will cause an error")
```

Here, the missing colon after **True** results in a **SyntaxError**. To fix this, simply add the colon:

```
if True:
    print("This works now!")
```

Unmatched parentheses are another common issue. Parentheses must always be properly closed, like securing the straps of your backpack before heading deeper into the jungle. A single unclosed parenthesis can unravel your entire journey:

```
print("Hello, World!"
```

The missing closing parenthesis causes a **SyntaxError**. Correcting it is straightforward:

```
print("Hello, World!")
```

These errors are easy to make, especially in longer, more complex code. But with vigilance, you can avoid them, keeping your journey on track.

Hidden Pitfalls: Incorrect Indentation

In Python, indentation is not just about making your code look neat—it defines the structure of your code blocks. Incorrect indentation is like a hidden pitfall in the jungle floor, ready to swallow you whole if you're not careful.

Consider this example:

```
def say_hello():
print("Hello, there!")
```

The lack of proper indentation under the **def** statement triggers an **IndentationError**. By correctly indenting the **print** line, the code functions as expected:

```
def say_hello():
    print("Hello, there!")
```

Mixing tabs and spaces or inconsistent indentation levels can also lead to errors. Ensuring consistent indentation throughout your code is crucial to avoid these pitfalls.

The Camouflaged Threat: Misspelled Keywords or Variable Names

Misspelled keywords or variable names are like camouflaged predators, lurking in the shadows, waiting to strike when you least expect it. Python's case sensitivity means that even a small typo can cause issues. For instance:

```
pritn("Oops, that's a typo!")
```

The above code prompts a **NameError** because **pritn** is not recognized. Correcting the typo resolves the error:

```
print("That's better!")
```

To solidify these concepts, practicing error correction is essential. Let's walk through some exercises to apply what we've learned.

Exercises: Clearing the Path

Exercise 1: Identifying Missing Colons

Review the code below and identify the syntax error:

```
for i in range(5)
    print(i)
```

Solution: The missing colon after **range(5)** needs to be added:

```python
for i in range(5):
    print(i)
```

Exercise 2: Fixing Unmatched Parentheses

Identify the issue in the following code:

```python
numbers = [1, 2, 3, 4, 5
print(numbers)
```

Solution: Close the list with a closing bracket:

```python
numbers = [1, 2, 3, 4, 5]
print(numbers)
```

Exercise 3: Correcting Indentation Errors

Spot the indentation mistake here:

```python
def greet(name):
print(f"Hello, {name}")
```

Solution: Indent the print statement:

```python
def greet(name):
    print(f"Hello, {name}")
```

Exercise 4: Rectifying Misspelled Keywords

Find the typo in this code snippet:

```python
def my_function():
    reurn "Nope, that's a typo!"
```

Solution: Correct the spelling of **return**:

```
def my_function():
    return "All fixed!"
```

With these exercises, you clear the path through the underbrush, but the deeper you go, the more dangerous the jungle becomes. It's time to face the next challenge.

The Quicksand of Execution Errors

As you venture deeper into the jungle, you encounter treacherous quicksand—execution errors. These errors occur during runtime, often catching you off guard. Understanding how certain operations can cause disruptions, such as division by zero, accessing undefined variables, or using out-of-range indices, is critical. Let's explore practical methods to resolve runtime errors effectively.

The Sinking Feeling: Division by Zero

One common type of runtime error is caused by performing an illegal operation, such as dividing a number by zero. This is like stepping into quicksand—your program will halt immediately, leaving you stuck.

Consider the following code snippet in Python:

```
def main():
    a = 5
    try:
        print(a / 0)
    except ZeroDivisionError as e:
        print(f"Error: {e}")

if __name__ == "__main__":
    main()
```

In this example, attempting to divide the variable **a** by zero raises a **ZeroDivisionError**, which is gracefully handled within a **try-except** block. This prevents the program from crashing and provides a meaningful error message to the user.

The Hidden Sinkhole: Accessing Undefined Variables or Out-Of-Range Indices

Another frequent runtime issue arises when code attempts to access a variable that hasn't been defined or tries to use an index that lies outside the bounds of a list or array. These errors are like hidden sinkholes, ready to swallow your program whole.

Consider this example where an array index is accessed out of range:

```python
pythonCopy codenumbers = [1, 2, 3]
print(numbers[3])   # Accessing out-of-bounds index
```

In this case, trying to access **numbers[3]** will result in an **IndexError** because the valid indices for this array are 0, 1, and 2. Always ensure indices are within the permissible range to avoid such pitfalls.

The Poisonous Plants: Inappropriate Data Types or Invalid Function Arguments

Type mismatches and invalid arguments passed to functions are another source of runtime errors. These are like poisonous plants in the jungle—seemingly harmless, but deadly if mishandled.

For example, let's examine a simple function designed to compute the square root of a number in Python:

```python
import math

def compute_square_root(value):
    if not isinstance(value, (int, float)):
        raise TypeError("Value must be an integer or float")
    if value < 0:
        raise ValueError("Cannot compute square root of a negative number")
    return math.sqrt(value)

try:
    result = compute_square_root(-9)
    print(result)
except (TypeError, ValueError) as e:
    print(f"Error: {e}")
```

Here, the function **compute_square_root** checks if the input value is either an integer or float and whether it is nonnegative before computing its square root. Both type and value validations help catch improper inputs early, preventing the function from executing incorrectly or crashing.

Transition to Logical Errors

Once you have a good handle on syntax and runtime errors, it's time to tackle the more elusive logical errors. These errors don't always cause immediate crashes, but they can lead your code astray, producing incorrect results or unexpected behavior. Understanding and fixing logical errors is where your debugging skills will truly be put to the test.

The Mirages: Logic Errors

As you go further into the jungle, you begin to encounter mirages—logic errors. These errors are the most insidious of all because they don't trigger visible crashes but lead to incorrect results. Correcting logical flaws in your code is crucial to ensure it behaves as expected.

The Mirage of Incorrect Logic

Logical errors typically arise when the program executes without encountering any syntax or runtime errors but still produces unintended outcomes. For instance, consider a function designed to calculate the average of a list of numbers. If the logic for computing the average mistakenly divides the sum of the list by the total sum again instead of the number of elements, the code runs without errors but returns an incorrect result.

To identify such logical errors, you must meticulously compare the expected output against the actual output and understand the intended functionality of each part of your code.

The Labyrinth of Loops and Conditionals

These foundational constructs are the lifeblood of most algorithms, allowing you to repeat actions, make decisions, and control the flow of your programs. However, as with any powerful tool, they come with their own set of challenges. Missteps in the logic of loops and conditionals can lead to subtle and elusive bugs, making them a common source of frustration for both novice and experienced coders alike.

Understanding the Complexity: Why Loops and Conditionals Are Tricky

Loops and conditionals are deceptively simple in concept. A loop repeatedly executes a block of code, while conditionals allow different blocks of code to execute based on certain conditions. Yet, their simplicity can be misleading. Even minor mistakes in their implementation can lead to significant and hard-to-find errors, often referred to as "logical bugs."

Consider the importance of getting the loop boundaries right. In a **for** loop, for instance, it's easy to make an off-by-one error—either including one too many iterations or one too few. Imagine you're tasked with processing every element in an array, but due to an off-by-one error, the loop skips the last element. This might happen if the loop's termination condition is incorrectly set. Instead of running from 0 to **length - 1**, it might run from 0 to **length**, leading to either an attempt to access an out-of-bounds index or an incomplete processing of the array elements.

Conditionals, on the other hand, introduce their own set of complexities. Nested conditionals, while powerful, can easily lead to conflicting logic paths. For example, consider a series of **if-else** statements designed to check multiple conditions. If these conditions overlap in ways not immediately obvious, you might end up with code that behaves unpredictably depending on the specific values encountered at runtime. This kind of problem is particularly tricky because it often only surfaces under specific circumstances, making it difficult to replicate and debug.

Case 1: The Off-By-One Error

Let's dive into a specific case to understand how these errors can manifest in real-world scenarios. Imagine you're writing a function to sum the values of all elements in an array:

```python
def sum_array(arr):
    total = 0
    for i in range(len(arr)):
        total += arr[i]
    return total
```

At first glance, this code seems perfectly fine. The loop runs from 0 to **len(arr) - 1**, adding each element of the array to **total**. However, what if the array is empty? The **len(arr)** would be 0, and thus, the loop wouldn't execute at all. While this behavior is correct, what if the loop's index variable, **i**, was mistakenly used in a different context, such as referencing an element outside the loop?

Imagine this:

```python
def sum_array(arr):
    total = 0
    for i in range(len(arr)):
        total += arr[i]
    print(f"Last element processed: {arr[i]}")
    return total
```

Here, the **print** statement tries to access **arr[i]** after the loop completes. If the array length is 3, **i** would be 2 after the last iteration. But post-loop, i would be 3, which is out-of-bounds, leading to an **IndexError**. This type of bug, an off-by-one error, is common and can easily slip through initial testing if not carefully considered.

Case 2: The Nested Conditional Trap

Another case study involves nested conditionals that lead to conflicting logic. Consider a system that determines eligibility for a service based on age and income:

```
def check_eligibility(age, income):
    if age > 18:
        if income > 50000:
            return "Eligible"
        else:
            return "Not eligible"
    else:
        if income < 20000:
            return "Eligible"
        else:
            return "Not eligible"
```

At first glance, this nested conditional logic seems reasonable. But what happens when age is exactly 18 or when income is exactly 50,000 or 20,000? The logic may not handle these edge cases as expected, leading to confusing outcomes.

For example, if age is 18 and income is 30,000, the function might return, "Not eligible," but if age is 18 and income is 15,000, it could return, "Eligible." This is because the logic paths are not mutually exclusive and the edge conditions have not been explicitly defined.

This kind of error can be avoided by carefully planning out the decision tree and ensuring that every possible path has been considered. Rewriting the function with clear and explicit conditions can help:

```
def check_eligibility(age, income):
    if age > 18 and income > 50000:
        return "Eligible"
    elif age <= 18 and income < 20000:
        return "Eligible"
    else:
        return "Not eligible"
```

Here, the conditions are laid out more clearly, and the logic paths are simplified, reducing the risk of conflicting outcomes.

Case 3: Infinite Loops and Logical Fallacies

Infinite loops are another common pitfall when working with loops and conditionals. Consider the following scenario where you're tasked with writing a loop that continues processing user input until a valid value is entered:

```
def get_valid_input():
    while True:
        user_input = input("Enter a number greater than 10: ")
        if int(user_input) > 10:
            break
    return int(user_input)
```

In this case, the loop is designed to continue prompting the user until they enter a valid number. However, imagine what happens if the user enters a nonnumeric value, such as "abc." The int(user_input) conversion will throw a **ValueError**, and the program will crash. The loop never gets a chance to correct the user's input, leading to a poor user experience and a broken program.

To fix this, you need to add error handling within the loop:

```
def get_valid_input():
    while True:
        user_input = input("Enter a number greater than 10: ")
        try:
            if int(user_input) > 10:
                break
        except ValueError:
            print("Please enter a valid number.")
    return int(user_input)
```

This updated version includes a **try-except** block to handle nonnumeric inputs gracefully. By catching the **ValueError**, the loop can continue to prompt the user until a valid input is provided.

The Importance of Testing

Developing techniques to test and verify the accuracy of algorithm implementations is another critical step. Unit testing stands out as an essential method for validating individual components of your program. By isolating and testing small, manageable pieces of code, you can ensure each segment functions correctly. Writing comprehensive unit tests for various scenarios, including edge cases, allows you to pinpoint where logical errors might be hiding.

Implementing automated tests using frameworks like **unittest** in Python ensures consistent and thorough testing across diverse code sections. This practice is your beacon, guiding you through the labyrinth and helping you stay on course.

The Tools of Survival: Debugging Tools and Techniques

To survive the jungle, you need the right tools. Effectively using tools and strategies to trace and fix code issues is essential for any programmer. Let's discuss several techniques, starting with the application of print statements.

The Machete: Print Statements

Print statements are often the first line of defense in debugging. By inserting **print** functions at key points in your code, you can inspect variable values and trace program execution steps. For example, if a function isn't producing the expected output, you might add **print(variable_name)** before and after the variable changes to see where things go wrong. This simple method allows you to quickly identify the state of your program at various stages.

The Compass: Built-in Debugging Tools

However, print statements have limitations, especially in more extensive or complex codebases. This is where built-in Python debugging tools like **pdb** come into play. **pdb**, Python's built-in debugger, offers a more sophisticated way to step through your code and set breakpoints. A breakpoint is a designated spot in your code where execution will pause, allowing you to inspect what's happening. You can initiate **pdb** by inserting **import pdb; pdb.set_trace()** at the desired point. Once the program hits this line, it drops into an interactive mode where you can evaluate expressions, move up and down the call stack, and continue execution line by line. This tool is invaluable for dissecting why certain parts of your code are behaving unexpectedly.

The Shield: Error Handling

Handling runtime errors gracefully using **try** and **except** blocks is like having a shield to protect you from the unexpected dangers lurking in the jungle. These blocks allow you to manage exceptions smoothly without crashing your application.

For example, if your program attempts to read a file that doesn't exist, a **try-except** block can catch the resulting **FileNotFoundError** and provide a user-friendly message instead of terminating:

```python
try:
    with open('data.txt') as f:
        data = f.read()
except FileNotFoundError:
    print("The file was not found.")
```

Proper error handling not only makes your programs more resilient but also aids in diagnosing and debugging issues when they arise.

The Final Chamber: Confronting the Final Boss: Error Entity

At the heart of this coding jungle lies the ultimate challenge—Error Entity. This Final Boss embodies the most complex and elusive bugs, combining elements of syntax errors, runtime errors, and logical errors. To defeat this mythical creature, you must bring together all the principles and tools you've learned and apply them to a large, buggy script or project.

The Error Entity thrives in large, complex systems where bugs can be deeply hidden and interconnected. To defeat it, you must dissect the entire project, hunting down errors with precision and skill.

Step 1: Dissecting the Buggy Script

Begin by analyzing the project as a whole. Identify the areas where bugs are most likely to occur—complex functions, nested loops, or areas with heavy data processing. Use your knowledge of common syntax and runtime errors to quickly spot the most obvious issues. For example:

```
def process_data(data):
    for item in data:
        if item not None:  # Missing 'is' keyword
            print(item)
```

Correct the syntax errors first. In this case, add the missing **is** keyword:

```
def process_data(data):
    for item in data:
        if item is not None:
            print(item)
```

Step 2: Handling Runtime Errors

Next, focus on runtime errors. Look for operations that could cause the program to crash, such as division by zero or out-of-bounds indexing. Implement **try-except** blocks around these operations to handle them gracefully:

```
def calculate_average(values):
    try:
        return sum(values) / len(values)
```

```
    except ZeroDivisionError:
        return "Cannot calculate average for an empty list."
```

Step 3: Verifying Logic

Once the code runs without crashing, it's time to verify the logic. Test each function thoroughly to ensure it produces the expected results. Write unit tests to cover various input scenarios, including edge cases:

```
import unittest

class TestCalculations(unittest.TestCase):

    def test_average(self):
        self.assertEqual(calculate_average([1, 2, 3]), 2)
        self.assertEqual(calculate_average([]), "Cannot calculate average for an empty list.")

if __name__ == "__main__":
    unittest.main()
```

Step 4: Advanced Debugging Techniques

Finally, use advanced debugging tools like **pdb** to step through the code, set breakpoints, and inspect variables at different stages. If necessary, refactor the code to simplify complex functions or improve readability, making future debugging easier.

Phew! You fixed the final bug, and you defeated the Error Entity, emerging victorious from the coding jungle. The project runs smoothly, and you've demonstrated your proficiency in troubleshooting and problem-solving. You've learned to handle the complexities of large codebases, ensuring that your programs are robust, reliable, and maintainable.

As you leave the jungle behind, take a moment to reflect on the skills you've developed. Debugging is a lifelong journey in programming—each bug teaches you something new. Keep experimenting, keep testing, and keep refining your craft. Whether you're working on a small script or a massive application, the lessons from the coding jungle will always guide you.

CHAPTER 7

The Function Fields

Entering the Function Fields is like stepping into a vast, fertile landscape where every seed of logic you plant can grow into a powerful tool. Functions are the secret weapons in a programmer's toolkit, transforming repetitive tasks into flexible, reusable code snippets. Imagine if, every time you needed to greet someone or calculate an area, you had to write the code from scratch. Not only would this be tedious, but it would also be error-prone. Functions eliminate this repetition, making your code cleaner, more efficient, and easier to maintain.

The Foundation of the Fields: Defining Functions With Parameters and Return Values

The Function Fields are vast, and the foundation of everything in these fields is the ability to define and use functions effectively. Python functions are blocks of organized, reusable code that perform specific tasks. They improve code readability, promote reusability, and make the development process more manageable and less error-prone. Understanding how to define and use functions is essential for anyone who wishes to harness the full power of the Function Fields.

Planting the Seeds: Learning to Use the def Keyword

In Python, functions are defined using the **def** keyword, which is like planting a seed in the Function Fields. This keyword is followed by the function name and parentheses, which may contain parameters. Parameters are inputs to the function that allow it to operate on different data without altering its structure.

Here's a simple example:

```python
def greet(name):
    print(f"Hello, {name}!")
```

In this snippet, we've planted a seed named **greet** that takes one parameter, **name**. When you call this function and pass an argument (like **"Alice"**), it prints a greeting message. Calling **greet('Alice')** would output **Hello, Alice!**.

But why stop at one seed? Functions can have multiple parameters, enabling them to perform more complex tasks. Consider a function that calculates the area of a rectangle:

```python
def area(length, width):
    return length * width
```

Here, **area(5, 3)** would return **15**, which is the area of a rectangle with a length of 5 and a width of 3.

Nurturing Growth: Passing Parameters Into Functions

Parameters are like the nutrients that feed your seeds, making your functions dynamic and versatile. When defining a function, you can specify default values for parameters. Default values allow the function to be called with fewer arguments than specified. For example:

```python
def greet(name="Guest"):
    print(f"Hello, {name}!")
```

In this case, calling **greet()** without any arguments would output **Hello, Guest!**, while calling **greet('Bob')** would output **Hello, Bob!**. Default values make your functions more flexible and user-friendly, allowing them to adapt to different situations.

But what if you don't know how many nutrients (parameters) your function might need? Python supports variable-length arguments, where you don't need to know beforehand how many arguments will be passed. Using an asterisk * before a parameter allows you to handle an arbitrary number of positional arguments:

```python
def sum_all(*nums):
    return sum(nums)
```

Calling **sum_all(1, 2, 3, 4)** would return **10**, as it sums up all the passed numbers. This ability to adapt to varying inputs is what makes the Function Fields so rich and productive.

Harvesting the Crops: Understanding Return Values

Return values are the crops you harvest from your well-tended fields. The **return** statement sends a result back to the caller and terminates the function's execution. Returning values allows the calling code to use the results for further processing.

For example:

```
def add(a, b):
    return a + b
```

Calling **result = add(2, 3)** stores the value **5** in the variable **result**. Without a return value, the function might just execute its internal code but wouldn't provide any output back to the caller, limiting its usefulness.

```
def no_return_add(a, b):
    summation = a + b

result = no_return_add(2, 3)   # result will be None
```

Tending to the Fields: The Importance of Clear and Descriptive Function Names

Just as a farmer needs clear labels to identify crops, naming functions clearly and descriptively is crucial. Function names should convey their purpose without needing additional explanation. This practice enhances code readability and maintainability.

Compare these two examples:

```
def x(a, b):
    return a + b
```

versus

```
def add_numbers(a, b):
    return a + b
```

The second example clearly states what the function does, making the code easier to understand and maintain. Using conventions such as **snake_case** for function names (e.g., **calculate_area**, **send_email**) aligns with widely accepted Python coding standards, contributing to consistent and readable code.

The Fields in Bloom: Best Practices

Now that we've planted the seeds, nurtured them, and understood how to harvest the crops, let's see the Function Fields in full bloom. Here are some practical examples that demonstrate how functions can be used effectively.

Example 1: Calculating the Area of a Circle

Let's define a function that calculates the area of a circle:

```python
def calculate_circle_area(radius):
    """Calculate the area of a circle given its radius."""
    import math
    return math.pi * radius ** 2
```

Using the function:

```python
circle_area = calculate_circle_area(5)
print(f"The area of the circle is: {circle_area}")
```

This example not only defines a function but also includes a docstring (a string literal at the beginning of the function body) that explains what the function does. Including docstrings is considered good practice because they offer valuable context for anyone reading the code later, whether it's yourself or another developer.

Example 2: Flexible Contact Details

Let's create a function that prints contact details, allowing for an optional email parameter:

```python
def contact_details(name, phone, email=None):
    details = f"Name: {name}\nPhone: {phone}"
    if email:
        details += f"\nEmail: {email}"
    return details
```

Calling the function with and without the optional email parameter:

```
print(contact_details("Alice", "123-456-7890"))
print(contact_details("Bob", "098-765-4321", "bob@example.com"))
```

By providing the email parameter with a default value of **None**, we maintain flexibility in how the function can be used.

The Boundaries of the Fields: Understanding Function Scope

The Function Fields are vast, but they have boundaries—these boundaries are defined by the scope and lifetime of variables within functions. Understanding scope is fundamental to mastering Python and writing modular, efficient code.

The Local Farm: Local and Global Variables

In Python, a local variable is one that is declared inside a function and can only be accessed within that function. On the other hand, a global variable is declared outside any function and can be accessed by any function within the same module.

Consider this example:

```
x = 10  # Global variable

def my_function():
    y = 20  # Local variable
    print(x)  # Accessing global variable
    print(y)

my_function()
print(x)
# print(y) would cause an error because y is not defined outside my_function
```

Here, **x** is a global variable, and **y** is a local variable. The local variable **y** can only be accessed within **my_function**, while the global variable **x** can be accessed both inside and outside **my_function**. Understanding this distinction is crucial because it helps prevent unintended side effects and makes the code more predictable and easier to debug.

The LEGB Law of the Land: Scope Affects Function Behavior

The scope of a variable directly influences the behavior of functions. When a variable is referenced within a function, Python first searches for it in the local scope. If it doesn't find it there, it then searches in the enclosing scopes, up to the global scope. This search mechanism is known as the LEGB rule—Local, Enclosing, Global, Built-in—which defines the order in which Python looks for variables.

Consider this example:

```python
x = "global"

def outer_function():
    x = "enclosed"

    def inner_function():
        x = "local"
        print("Inner:", x)

    inner_function()
    print("Outer:", x)

outer_function()
print("Global:", x)
```

The output will be:

```
Inner: local
Outer: enclosed
Global: global
```

This demonstrates how Python resolves variable names based on their scope. The **inner_function** prints the value of **x** from its local scope, while **outer_function** prints the value from its enclosed scope, and the global scope remains unaffected by these changes.

Avoiding Weeds: Best Practices for Variable Naming

To avoid conflicts and ensure clarity in your code, it's essential to follow best practices for variable naming. Use descriptive names that indicate the variable's purpose, such as **user_count** or **total_amount**. Avoid using single-letter variable names except for loop counters. Ensuring that variable names are unique within their respective scopes helps prevent shadowing, where a local variable hides a global variable with the same name.

For instance:

```
count = 5  # Global variable

def increment_count():
    count = 10  # Local variable, shadows the global 'count'
    count += 1
    print(count)  # Prints: 11

increment_count()
print(count)  # Prints: 5
```

In this case, the local variable **count** within **increment_count** shadows the global variable **count**, leading to potential confusion if not properly managed.

Going Deeper: Recursive Functions and Lambda Expressions

In the farthest reaches of the Function Fields lie some advanced concepts—recursion and lambda expressions. Understanding these will help you write more compact, efficient code, enhancing your ability to create sophisticated programs.

The Self-Sustaining Crop: Recursive Functions

Recursion is a technique where a function calls itself to solve a problem. This can simplify complex problems by breaking them down into smaller subproblems of the same type. One classic example of recursion is calculating the Fibonacci sequence, where each number is the sum of the two preceding ones. The recursive approach to this problem is elegant and concise.

For instance, consider the Fibonacci sequence written recursively:

```
def fibonacci(n):
    if n <= 0:
        return 0
    elif n == 1:
        return 1
    else:
        return fibonacci(n-1) + fibonacci(n-2)
```

This code snippet defines a function **fibonacci** that returns the nth Fibonacci number. The function calls itself with decremented values until it reaches the base cases (**n <= 0** or **n == 1**). Recursion is particularly useful in scenarios that naturally fit a divide-and-conquer strategy, such as sorting algorithms like **quicksort** and **merge sort**, and in problems related to mathematical computations, tree traversal, or graph algorithms.

However, it's important to note that recursion can lead to excessive use of memory and slower performance for large datasets due to the overhead of function calls and the stack space required. Managing recursion carefully, perhaps using techniques like memoization, can help mitigate some of these issues.

The Quick Sprout: Lambda Expressions

Lambda expressions are a way to create small, anonymous functions in Python. Lambdas can take any number of arguments but only one expression. Unlike regular functions defined using **def**, lambdas are written in a single line and do not require a name. This makes them ideal for short operations that are not going to be reused elsewhere in your code.

Here's a basic example of a lambda function that squares a number:

```
square = lambda x: x * x
print(square(5))
```

The output will be **25**. Although simple, this demonstrates how lambdas can be compact yet powerful. They are often used in conjunction with functions like **map()**, **filter()**, and **reduce()** which perform operations on lists or other iterable structures.

Consider the use of lambda with the **filter()** function to filter out elements from a list that don't meet a certain condition. For example:

```
numbers = [1, 2, 3, 4, 5, 6]
even_numbers = list(filter(lambda x: x % 2 == 0, numbers))
print(even_numbers)
```

This produces [2, 4, 6], showing how lambda functions provide an elegant solution for inline operations without the verbosity of defining separate named functions.

Lambda functions also lend themselves well to scenarios needing function shorthand within higher-order functions. As an example, let's look at the **map()** function, which applies a given function to all items in an input list:

```
numbers = [1, 2, 3, 4, 5]
squared_numbers = list(map(lambda x: x * x, numbers))
print(squared_numbers)
```

This outputs [1, 4, 9, 16, 25], effectively squaring each number in the original list. The utility of lambdas here lies in their brevity and clarity, making the code easier to read and maintain.

Another practical example is using lambdas with the **reduce()** function, found in the **functools** module, to apply a rolling computation to sequential pairs of values in a list:

```
from functools import reduce

numbers = [1, 2, 3, 4, 5]
product = reduce(lambda x, y: x * y, numbers)
print(product)
```

This calculates the product of all elements in the list, producing **120**. The lambda function succinctly defines the multiplication operation without requiring a separate function definition.

Combining recursion with lambda functions can lead to very succinct but complex code. Here's an advanced example where the Fibonacci sequence is calculated using a lambda expression recursively:

```
fibonacci_lambda = lambda n: n if n <= 1 else fibonacci_lambda(n-1) +
fibonacci_lambda(n-2)
print(fibonacci_lambda(5))
```

Though elegant, recursive lambda functions should be used with caution due to potential readability and debugging challenges.

The DRY Principle: Avoiding Repetition in the Fields

When tending to your fields, repetition can lead to a barren land, overgrown with unnecessary complexity. The DRY principle—Don't Repeat Yourself—is a cornerstone in promoting reusable and modular code. Adhering to the DRY principle allows you to create Python programs that are not only efficient but also easier to manage and extend over time.

Why Repetition Is Problematic

Repeating code, especially large chunks of it, leads to what can be termed "maintenance debt." Imagine you have three similar functions: **doStuff1**, **doStuff2**, and **doStuff3**. If a bug is discovered in one function, you'll need to remember to fix it in all three. This increases the likelihood of errors because it's easy to overlook one or more instances of the duplicated logic. Furthermore, should any new functionality be added, every place where the duplicated code exists must be updated, leading to increased effort and potential inconsistencies.

To combat this, break down tasks into small, reusable functions. Each function should perform a single task and perform it well. For instance, instead of three nearly identical **doStuff** functions, create one versatile function that accepts parameters to handle different cases. This approach not only eliminates redundancy but also fosters the development of cleaner, more readable code.

Consider this refactoring:

- Before:

```
def doStuff1():
    # do something

def doStuff2():
    # do the same thing with slight variation

def doStuff3():
    # do the same thing with another slight variation
```

- After:

```
def do_stuff(variation):
    if variation == 1:
        # do something
    elif variation == 2:
        # do the same thing with slight variation
    elif variation == 3:
        # do the same thing with another slight variation
```

By consolidating the functionality into one versatile function, you eliminate repetition and simplify the maintenance of your code.

The Power of Modular Code

Modular code shines when maintaining and reading codebases. Modular designs encapsulate functionality within self-contained units, making it easier to see what each part does without wading through unrelated code. Consider the difference between a lengthy unstructured script and a well-organized module with clear, purpose-specific functions. The latter is inherently easier to read, debug, and modify.

A practical example of modular code improving maintainability can be seen in utility functions. Suppose you're working on a project involving data processing. You might find certain operations—like parsing input files, cleaning data, or generating reports—tend to repeat. Instead of embedding these operations throughout your code, encapsulate them in utility functions. This separation allows you to call a single utility function whenever needed, enhancing clarity and reducing the room for error.

For example:

```python
def clean_data(data):
    # clean data

def parse_file(file_path):
    data = open(file_path).read()
    return clean_data(data)

def generate_report(cleaned_data):
    # generate report from cleaned data
```

By creating modular utility functions, you make your codebase more organized and easier to maintain.

The Final Boss: Function Fiend

The journey through the Function Fields has brought you far, but now it's time to face the ultimate challenge—the Function Fiend. This final boss tests your ability to develop a functional module or library that solves a complex problem, such as data processing or mathematical computations. To defeat this foe, you'll need to apply all the principles you've learned—modularity, reusability, recursion, and lambda expressions—to create a robust solution.

Imagine you're tasked with processing a large dataset containing thousands of records. Your challenge is to read data from files, filter or transform the data, and generate various reports. The Function Fiend will try to overwhelm you with complexity, but by encapsulating all related functions within a module, you can build a reusable package that will help you conquer this challenge.

Here's a simple guideline for developing such a module:

1. **Identify the core functionalities** required by your module (e.g., read data, process data, or output results).

2. **Define a clear application programming interface (API)** for your module, making it easy for others (and future you) to utilize its functions.

3. **Document your code**, providing examples of how each function should be used.

4. **Test thoroughly** to ensure reliability and handle edge cases gracefully.

Suppose we are developing a data processing module:

```python
# data_processing.py

def read_data(file_path):
    with open(file_path, 'r') as f:
        data = f.readlines()
    return data

def process_data(data):
    processed = [line.strip() for line in data if line.strip()]
    return processed

def output_results(processed_data, output_file):
    with open(output_file, 'w') as f:
        for item in processed_data:
            f.write(f"{item}\n")
```

By organizing your code into a module, you make it more manageable, testable, and reusable. Not only does this approach streamline your current project, but it also lays the groundwork for future endeavors, allowing you to build upon existing work without reinventing the wheel.

Congratulations! You've defeated the Function Fiend. Your ability to create efficient and modular code has grown stronger, enabling you to handle more complex programming challenges with confidence. You're ready to continue with your adventure.

CHAPTER 8

The Modules Mountain

The path up Modules Mountain is daunting. You've already conquered the basics, but now, as you stare at the towering peak above, you know this will be your greatest test yet. It's a place where only the most dedicated programmers dare to tread, for it is here that you will master the art of managing Python's powerful modules and libraries, learning to wield them with the precision of a seasoned coder.

The Beginning of the Ascent

The climb begins with a familiar trail—the Standard Library Trail—a path well-worn by many who have come before you. The early morning sun filters through the trees, casting dappled light on the ground as you make your way forward. This is the foundation of every Python coder's journey, and you tread with confidence, ready to uncover the secrets that lie ahead.

The Standard Library Trail

As you walk, the first guide you encounter is **os**, a traveler of the mountain. He's a practical, no-nonsense companion who teaches you how to interact with the operating system—an essential skill for any developer.

"Need to manage files? Navigate directories? Execute system commands? I can help you with that," **os** says, handing you a map filled with commands.

- Creating directories:

```
import os
os.mkdir('new_directory')
```

- Listing files in a directory:

```
files = os.listdir('.')
print(files)
```

- Renaming files:

```
os.rename('old_name.txt', 'new_name.txt')
```

These commands flow easily, and you can already see how you might use them to automate tedious tasks, organize files, and more. With **os** by your side, you move deeper into the mountain.

Next, you meet **sys**, a methodical and precise guide who specializes in system-specific parameters and functions. He offers tools that are invaluable for scripting and automation.

- Accessing command-line arguments:

```
import sys
print(sys.argv)
```

- Exiting a program:

```
import sys
sys.exit("Exiting the program due to an error.")
```

Sys's tools allow your scripts to adapt to different environments, making them more flexible and robust. As you follow his lead, you understand that sys is a critical part of any serious Python programmer's toolkit.

As the trail ascends, you encounter **Datetime**, a calm and measured presence who introduces you to time itself. With Datetime's help, you learn how to manipulate time with precision, whether for scheduling tasks, logging events, or handling time zones.

- Getting the current date and time:

```
from datetime import datetime
now = datetime.now()
print(now)
```

- Formatting dates:

```
formatted_date = now.strftime("%Y-%m-%d %H:%M:%S")
print(formatted_date)
```

- Calculating time differences:

```
from datetime import timedelta
future_date = now + timedelta(days=5)
print(future_date)
```

With these new skills, your scripts can now operate with the precision of a clock, timing actions perfectly and recording events with accuracy. As you continue up the mountain, the tools of the Standard Library fill your backpack, each one a valuable resource for the challenges ahead.

Venturing Into the PyPI Forest

The trail eventually leads you to a dense, vibrant forest—the PyPI Forest—a place teeming with life and possibilities. This is where countless third-party libraries reside, offering specialized tools and capabilities that go beyond what the Standard Library can provide.

The forest is vast, and as you enter, you are immediately met by **Requests**, a friendly and knowledgeable guide. "If you need to interact with web services or make HTTP requests, I'm your library," she says, her tone reassuring.

- Making a GET request:

```
import requests
response = requests.get('https://api.example.com/data')
if response.status_code == 200:
    print(response.json())
else:
    print("Failed to retrieve data.")
```

Requests teaches you how to fetch data from the web effortlessly, turning complex tasks into simple ones. Whether you're working with APIs or scraping web content, Requests makes the process smooth and manageable.

As you venture further, you encounter **NumPy**, a formidable figure who introduces you to the world of numerical computing. NumPy is powerful, capable of handling large datasets and performing complex mathematical operations with ease.

- Creating and manipulating arrays:

```
import numpy as np
array = np.array([1, 2, 3, 4, 5])
print(array * 2)  # Outputs: [2 4 6 8 10]
```

- Advanced operations:

```
matrix = np.array([[1, 2], [3, 4]])
transposed = np.transpose(matrix)
print(transposed)
```

With NumPy, you see the potential for advanced data analysis, machine learning, and scientific computing. Your mind races with ideas for how you might use these tools in your projects.

Moving deeper into the forest, you meet other valuable companions—**Pandas**, who helps you manage and analyze complex datasets, and **Matplotlib**, who shows you how to visualize data in meaningful ways.

- Using pandas for DataFrames:

```
import pandas as pd
data = {'Name': ['Alex', 'Jordan', 'Taylor'], 'Age': [25, 30, 22]}
df = pd.DataFrame(data)
print(df)
```

- Creating a simple plot with Matplotlib:

```
import matplotlib.pyplot as plt
plt.plot([1, 2, 3], [4, 5, 6])
plt.xlabel('X-axis')
```

```
plt.ylabel('Y-axis')
plt.title('Simple Plot')
plt.show()
```

As you gather these tools, your confidence grows. You're now capable of handling a wide range of tasks—from fetching and processing data to visualizing it in ways that convey meaning and insight. But with great power comes great responsibility, and you soon realize that the more tools you have, the more important it is to manage them effectively.

Crafting Custom Modules

The trail becomes steeper as you ascend, but you're determined to keep moving forward. Soon, you reach a forge nestled within the mountain—the Custom Modules Forge. Here, you learn how to craft your own tools, creating custom modules that encapsulate your most-used functions and classes.

The forge master, Artisan Py, welcomes you warmly. "Here, you can craft modules to organize your code and make it reusable across projects," he explains, his hands deftly shaping raw code into elegant, functional modules.

You decide to start simple. Perhaps a module to handle common string manipulations—a tool you've often found yourself rewriting in various projects.

• Creating a simple module:

```
# string_utils.py
def to_uppercase(s):
    """Converts a string to uppercase."""
    return s.upper()

def to_lowercase(s):
    """Converts a string to lowercase."""
    return s.lower()

def count_vowels(s):
    """Counts the number of vowels in a string."""
    return sum(1 for char in s.lower() if char in 'aeiou')
```

With Artisan Py's guidance, you craft your first custom module, organizing your code in a way that makes it easy to maintain and reuse. You can now import your module into any project, saving you time and effort.

- Using the custom module:

```
import string_utils
text = "Hello, World!"
print(string_utils.to_uppercase(text))  # Outputs: "HELLO, WORLD!"
print(string_utils.count_vowels(text))  # Outputs: 3
```

But you don't stop there. Inspired by the possibilities, you create more complex modules, each adapted to solve specific problems in your projects. Artisan Py shows you how to organize these modules into packages, grouping related functionalities together.

- Creating a package:

```
data_processing/
    __init__.py
    cleaning.py
    transformation.py
    visualization.py
```

The package you create is robust, a collection of tools that you can rely on in future projects. It's not just about saving time; it's about creating a library of solutions that grows with you as a developer. Each module, each package is a testament to your journey, a marker of how far you've come.

But as you prepare to leave the forge, Artisan Py offers a word of caution. "With power comes responsibility. As you create more modules and packages, managing them will become increasingly challenging. But fear not, for you are ready to face what lies ahead."

The Final Challenge: Facing the Module Minotaur

You've made it far, mastering both the tools provided by the Standard Library and those available in the PyPI Forest. You've even crafted your own modules, but the greatest challenge still lies ahead.

The air is thinner now, and the path is more treacherous. As you approach the summit, you find yourself at the entrance to a dark, winding labyrinth known as the Dependency Maze. It is here that many have faltered, unable to manage the complexities of integrating multiple modules and libraries into a single cohesive project.

As you step into the maze, the walls seem to close in around you. The paths twist and turn, leading to dead ends marked by version conflicts and compatibility issues. But you remain calm, knowing that you have the tools to navigate these challenges.

Your first step is to create a virtual environment, a haven within the maze where your project can reside, isolated from the global environment. This will protect your project from conflicting dependencies and ensure that all the modules you use are compatible with one another.

- Creating a virtual environment:

```
python -m venv myenv
```

- Activating the virtual environment:

```
# On Windows
myenv\Scripts\activate

# On Unix or macOS
source myenv/bin/activate
```

Within this environment, you carefully install the necessary libraries, specifying exact versions to avoid conflicts. Each library is like a stepping stone, guiding you further into the maze.

- Installing packages with specific versions:

```
pip install numpy==1.19.2
pip install pandas==1.1.3
```

With your environment set up and your dependencies managed, you venture deeper into the maze. But soon, you come face to face with the Module Minotaur—a fearsome creature representing the ultimate challenge of managing a complex project with multiple dependencies.

The Minotaur roars, attempting to overwhelm you with tangled dependencies, obscure errors, and incompatibilities. But you are prepared. You wield Pipenv, a powerful tool that combines the capabilities of pip and virtualenv, helping you manage dependencies with ease.

- Using pipenv to create and manage environments:

```
pip install pipenv
pipenv install requests
pipenv install numpy==1.19.2
```

Pipenv creates a **Pipfile** and **Pipfile.lock**, ensuring that all your dependencies are tracked and can be replicated consistently across different systems. This gives you confidence as you face the Minotaur, knowing that your project's environment is stable and controlled.

The Minotaur stumbles, but it is not defeated. It throws one final challenge—transitive dependencies and runtime errors designed to trip you up. These are the dependencies that your dependencies rely on, a tangled web that can easily become a nightmare if not managed carefully.

Undeterred, you call upon Docker, a tool that allows you to containerize your application, encapsulating the entire environment, including all dependencies, into a single, portable container. With Docker, you can run your application consistently across different environments, eliminating the risk of "it works on my machine" syndrome.

*   Creating a dockerfile:

```
# Use an official Python runtime as a parent image
FROM python:3.8-slim

# Set the working directory in the container
WORKDIR /app

# Copy the current directory contents into the container at /app
ADD . /app

# Install any needed packages specified in requirements.txt
RUN pip install --trusted-host pypi.python.org -r requirements.txt

# Make port 80 available to the world outside this container
EXPOSE 80

# Define environment variable
ENV NAME World

# Run app.py when the container launches
CMD ["python", "app.py"]
```

- Building and running the docker container:

```
docker build -t my-python-app .
docker run -p 4000:80 my-python-app
```

With Docker, you encapsulate everything—your code, your dependencies, even your environment. The Minotaur struggles as it realizes it can no longer disrupt your project. Your application runs smoothly, regardless of the host system, and the labyrinth begins to fade away.

As the Minotaur falls, you stand victorious. The challenges of Modules Mountain have been overcome, and you have emerged as a master of Python's modules and libraries.

The sky is clear as you finally reach the summit of Modules Mountain. You take a moment to breathe in the crisp air, reflecting on the journey that has brought you here. From the early steps on the Standard Library Trail to the deep explorations in the PyPI Forest, and the battles within the Dependency Maze, you have conquered each challenge with determination and skill.

At the summit, you understand that your journey is not truly over. The world of programming is vast and ever-changing, with new tools and challenges appearing all the time. But you are no longer a novice. You are a seasoned coder, capable of facing the complexities of Python's modules and libraries with confidence.

As you look out over the vast landscape below, you feel a deep sense of accomplishment. You know that whatever challenges lie ahead, you have the knowledge and tools to face them head-on.

Modules Mountain may have been a formidable challenge, but it is just one peak in the endless range of coding adventures. With your new skills, you are ready to tackle whatever comes next, whether it's scaling new heights, exploring uncharted territories, or helping others along their own journeys.

You smile, knowing that this is just the beginning of a lifetime of learning and discovery. The mountain has given you its treasures, and now, it's time to use them to create something truly remarkable.

CHAPTER 9

The Data Marketplace

The marketplace buzzes with energy. It's alive with the hum of countless transactions, the swirl of numbers, and the relentless flow of information. As you stand at the entrance, you know that this place holds immense power—power that can transform raw data into actionable insights. But to harness it, you must first learn to handle the data marketplace with skill and precision.

Entering the Marketplace

The first step is mastering the basics—learning how to read from and write to files. It's like setting up shop in the marketplace. Before you can start trading or making sense of what's around you, you need to establish your presence, gather your resources, and organize your tools.

Setting Up Shop: File Operations

You start with the simplest of tools, those that allow you to interact with text files. These are the foundational operations, the basics that will support everything you do from here on out.

- **Reading from a text file:** You find a small ledger—just a text file, really—and decide to see what it contains. Carefully, you use the tools at your disposal:

```
with open('example.txt', 'r') as file:
    content = file.read()
    print(content)
```

As the contents spill out in front of you, you realize how easy it is to access and read data. The **with** statement ensures that the file is properly closed after you're done, preventing any resource leaks—an important lesson you'll carry with you as you delve deeper into more complex data structures.

- **Writing to a text file:** Next, you decide to jot down some notes, adding your own entry to the marketplace's ledger:

```python
with open('example.txt', 'w') as file:
    file.write("Hello, data marketplace!")
```

Once again, the **with** statement ensures that everything is in order—no lingering processes, no locked files. You're starting to understand the importance of managing these resources carefully.

But the marketplace is vast, and text files are just the beginning. Soon, you'll need to handle more structured data, where simplicity won't suffice.

Exploring the Marketplace: CSV and Excel Files

The marketplace is full of more complex wares—tables, spreadsheets, datasets that require a more sophisticated touch. Here, you encounter CSV and Excel files, formats that are more structured and, consequently, more powerful.

- **Handling CSV files:** CSV files are like organized stalls in the marketplace, each row representing a transaction, each column a specific detail of that transaction. You decide to browse through one of these stalls:

```python
import csv

with open('data.csv', newline='') as csvfile:
    reader = csv.reader(csvfile)
    for row in reader:
        print(row)
```

The rows of data unfurl before you, each one a story waiting to be understood. But you're not just here to observe; you're here to trade, to manipulate the data as you see fit. You make a quick transaction, writing some new data into a CSV file:

```
data = [['Name', 'Age'], ['Alice', 30], ['Bob', 25]]

with open('output.csv', 'w', newline='') as csvfile:
    writer = csv.writer(csvfile)
    writer.writerows(data)
```

With a few lines of code, you've added a new entry to the marketplace, ready for others to explore.

- **Managing Excel files:** But CSV files are not the only treasures here. You spot an Excel spreadsheet—a more complex, but equally valuable, asset. Using the tools at your disposal, you decide to dig in:

```
import pandas as pd

# Reading from an Excel file
df = pd.read_excel('data.xlsx')
print(df.head())

# Writing to an Excel file
df.to_excel('output.xlsx', index=False)
```

The spreadsheet comes alive with data, neatly organized and easy to manipulate. You make some changes, add a few notes, and save it back in the marketplace for future use.

You're getting the hang of this—reading, writing, and manipulating data with ease. But the marketplace is more than just a place to gather data. It's a place to explore, analyze, and uncover hidden insights.

Navigating the Data Bazaar: Pandas

You've become comfortable with the basics, but now it's time to delve deeper. The marketplace has a bustling bazaar—a place where data is not just stored, but transformed. Here, you find **pandas**, remember them? That tool designed to help you make sense of the data before you.

The Power of DataFrames

In the heart of the bazaar, you encounter the **DataFrame**, pandas' primary data structure. It's like a versatile stall, capable of holding different types of goods—numbers, strings, even complex objects—each neatly arranged in columns and rows.

You start by setting up a stall of your own, loading data into a DataFrame:

```
import pandas as pd

df = pd.read_csv('market_data.csv')
print(df.head())
```

With a few simple commands, your stall is stocked with data, ready for analysis. But the real power of pandas lies in its ability to clean, manipulate, and transform this data.

Cleaning and Preparing Data

In the bazaar, cleanliness is paramount. No one wants to deal with dirty data, so you start by cleaning up your stall.

- **Handling missing values:** You notice some gaps in the data—missing values that could skew your analysis if left unchecked.

```
# Check for missing values
print(df.isnull().sum())

# Drop rows with missing values
df_cleaned = df.dropna()

# Fill missing values with a specific value
df_filled = df.fillna(0)
```

With the missing values addressed, your data is now cleaner and more reliable. But there's more work to be done.

- **Removing duplicates:** Duplicates are like counterfeit goods in the bazaar—unwanted and potentially harmful. You spot a few and decide to remove them:

```
# Identify duplicates
print(df.duplicated().sum())

# Remove duplicate rows
df_no_duplicates = df.drop_duplicates()
```

With the duplicates gone, your data is now pristine, ready for deeper analysis.

Manipulating and Analyzing Data

Now that your stall is in order, it's time to start trading—manipulating and analyzing the data to uncover hidden gems.

- **Filtering and grouping data:** You begin by filtering your wares, focusing on specific items that catch your eye:

```
# Filter rows where 'Price' is greater than 50
filtered_df = df[df['Price'] > 50]
```

- Next, you group similar items together, summarizing their values to gain insights into trends:

```
# Group by 'Category' and calculate the sum of 'Sales'
grouped = df.groupby('Category')['Sales'].sum()
```

The data starts to tell a story, one that reveals which items are selling the most, and which are lagging behind.

- **Merging DataFrames:** But your analysis is far from over. You decide to combine data from different stalls, merging them into a single, comprehensive view:

```
pythonCopy code# Merge two DataFrames on a common column 'ItemID'
merged_df = pd.merge(df1, df2, on='ItemID')
```

The merged data gives you a complete picture, one that spans across multiple aspects of the marketplace. You're starting to see the bigger picture, but there's still one more challenge to face.

The Final Boss: Facing the Data Dragon

As you explore the marketplace, you feel the ground tremble. The air grows thick with tension. You've heard the tales, and now you know them to be true—the Data Dragon resides here, deep within the marketplace, guarding the most valuable insights.

The Data Dragon is formidable, a creature that represents the ultimate challenge in data analysis. To defeat it, you must not only analyze and manipulate data but also extract meaningful insights and present them effectively.

Analyzing the Dataset

The Data Dragon's lair is filled with datasets—treasure troves of information waiting to be uncovered. You start by analyzing one of these datasets, using all the skills you've honed so far.

- **Exploratory data analysis:** You begin with exploratory data analysis, getting to know the dataset before you make any moves:

```
# Display the first few rows of the dataset
print(df.head())

# Summary statistics
print(df.describe())

# Information about the dataset
print(df.info())
```

As you sift through the data, patterns start to emerge—trends, anomalies, and relationships that hint at deeper insights.

Extracting Insights

The Data Dragon stirs, sensing your progress. But you're undeterred. Armed with your newfound knowledge, you dive deeper into the dataset, extracting insights that could turn the tide of battle.

- **Finding correlations:** You notice that some variables seem to be linked. To confirm your suspicions, you calculate the correlations:

```
# Calculate correlation matrix
correlation_matrix = df.corr()

# Print correlation matrix
print(correlation_matrix)
```

The correlations reveal relationships within the data—connections that might not have been obvious at first glance. These insights could be the key to defeating the Data Dragon.

Presenting the Insights

But analyzing the data is only half the battle. To truly defeat the Data Dragon, you must present your findings in a way that is clear, compelling, and actionable.

- **Visualizing the data:** You draw your weapon—Matplotlib—and prepare to visualize the data. Each plot is a strike against the Data Dragon, each visualization a step closer to victory.

  o **Line plots:** You start with a line plot, tracking changes over time:

```
import matplotlib.pyplot as plt

# Plotting a line graph
plt.plot(df['Date'], df['Sales'])
plt.title('Sales Over Time')
plt.xlabel('Date')
plt.ylabel('Sales')
plt.show()
```

The line plot reveals a clear trend, a pattern that could guide future decisions. But the Data Dragon is not so easily defeated.

  o **Bar charts:** Next, you create a bar chart, comparing different categories:

```
eimport seaborn as sns

# Creating a bar chart
sns.barplot(x='Category', y='Sales', data=df)
plt.title('Sales by Category')
plt.xlabel('Category')
plt.ylabel('Sales')
plt.show()
```

The bar chart brings clarity, showing which categories are thriving and which are struggling. The Data Dragon roars in frustration, but you press on.

  o **Heatmaps:** You follow up with a heatmap, uncovering relationships within the data:

```
# Creating a heatmap
sns.heatmap(df.corr(), annot=True, cmap='coolwarm')
plt.title('Correlation Heatmap')
plt.show()
```

The heatmap illuminates hidden connections, making them clear and actionable. The Data Dragon staggers, its defenses crumbling.

The Final Strike

The Data Dragon is weakened, but not yet defeated. You prepare for the final strike, drawing upon everything you've learned to craft a visualization that will end the battle once and for all.

- **Scatter plots:** You decide to create a scatter plot, highlighting the relationship between two key variables:

```python
# Creating a scatter plot
sns.scatterplot(x='Advertising Spend', y='Sales', data=df)
plt.title('Advertising Spend vs Sales')
plt.xlabel('Advertising Spend')
plt.ylabel('Sales')
plt.show()
```

> The scatter plot reveals a strong correlation, a relationship that could drive future strategies. The Data Dragon roars one last time, but it's too late. The final strike lands, and the beast falls.

As the dust settles, you stand victorious over the Data Dragon. The marketplace is quiet now, the tension gone. You've conquered the ultimate challenge, mastering the art of data analysis and presentation.

You take a moment to reflect on your journey. From learning the basics of file operations to navigating the complexities of pandas, from uncovering hidden insights to defeating the Data Dragon, you've come a long way.

But your journey is not over. The marketplace is vast, with new challenges and opportunities waiting just around the corner. Armed with your skills and knowledge, you're ready to face whatever comes next.

The marketplace is yours. Go forth and conquer.

CHAPTER 10

The API Abyss

The sea roils beneath you, dark and foreboding. The wind howls, and the sky is an endless sheet of stormy gray. But you stand firm, ready to go into the depths of the API Abyss. This is no ordinary voyage—this is where you will learn to command the power of APIs, bending the digital world to your will. Here, you will face challenges that test your ability to connect, retrieve, and manipulate data from the vast oceans of information that lie beyond the horizon. But with every storm comes clarity, and with every wave, an opportunity to master the seas.

Introducing APIs

APIs are your ship and compass in this vast, digital ocean. They allow you to go through the waters of data, connecting your application to external services, and bringing back the treasures of knowledge and functionality that lie beyond your immediate reach.

Imagine you are a captain, charting a course to an island where the richest resources lie. Without a map or a guide, your journey would be treacherous and uncertain. APIs serve as your navigational tools, guiding you through the software systems and allowing you to communicate effortlessly with them.

Setting Sail: Understanding APIs

To truly command the API Abyss, you first need to understand what APIs are and how they function. An API is a set of rules and protocols that allow different software applications to communicate with each other. It's like a trusted emissary who carries messages between kingdoms—each with its own language and customs—ensuring that everyone understands each other without revealing the inner workings of the kingdoms themselves.

In technical terms, an API specifies how software components should interact, defining the methods and data formats that can be used for communication. APIs are everywhere—from the social media platforms you use to the financial services you depend on. They allow you to connect your application to external systems, fetch data, send instructions, and much more.

Navigating the Seas: Making Your First API Call

With the basics in mind, it's time to set sail and make your first API call. In Python, the **requests** library is your anchor, providing a simple yet powerful way to interact with APIs. But before you can begin, you'll need to install the **requests** library. It's like equipping your ship with the necessary tools before you embark on your journey:

```
bashCopy codepip install requests
```

With your tools in hand, you can begin your voyage. Let's say you want to retrieve data from a distant API endpoint—perhaps you're curious about the current weather in a far-off city. You can make a request to the API as follows:

```
pythonCopy codeimport requests

response = requests.get('https://api.example.com/data')
```

This simple line of code sends an HTTP GET request to the specified URL. The server, like a wise oracle, processes your request and sends back a response. But how do you know if your request was successful? You check the response status code:

```
pythonCopy codeif response.status_code == 200:
    print('Request was successful!')
else:
    print('Request failed with status code:', response.status_code)
```

A status code of 200 indicates smooth sailing—a successful request. Other status codes, like 404 (Not Found) or 500 (Internal Server Error), indicate rough seas, where something has gone awry. Understanding these codes helps you diagnose problems quickly and adjust your course as needed.

Deciphering the Message: Handling JSON Responses

The data you retrieve from an API often comes in the form of JSON (short for JavaScript Object Notation), a lightweight and easy-to-read format that resembles a treasure map, guiding you to the information you seek. JSON is the preferred format for many APIs because it's both human-readable and machine-friendly.

Once you receive a JSON response, the next step is to decipher its contents and extract the valuable data within. In Python, this is as simple as converting the JSON-encoded content of a response to a Python dictionary:

```python
pythonCopy codejson_data = response.json()
print(json_data)
```

Now that the data is in a familiar format, you can easily navigate through it, accessing specific pieces of information like a seasoned explorer:

```python
pythonCopy codeuser_name = json_data['name']
user_email = json_data['email']
print(f"Name: {user_name}, Email: {user_email}")
```

With the data securely in your hands, you can integrate it into your application, turning raw information into actionable insights.

Exploring the Depths: Real-World Applications of APIs

As you venture deeper into the API Abyss, you'll discover that APIs are not just tools—they are gateways to a world of possibilities. APIs allow you to access and integrate a vast array of services, ranging from social media platforms to financial data streams, and even advanced artificial intelligence models.

- **Social media APIs:** Imagine building an application that keeps users updated with real-time social media posts. APIs like those from X (formerly Twitter) or Facebook allow you to fetch the latest posts and comments and display them in your app. You can also interact with these platforms by posting updates, liking content, or even following new accounts—all through the power of APIs.

- **Weather APIs:** For applications that rely on up-to-date weather information, APIs like OpenWeatherMap provide a wealth of meteorological data. Whether you're developing a travel app, an event planner, or even an agricultural tool, integrating a weather API can provide users with accurate forecasts, alerts, and historical data.

- **Financial APIs:** In finance, APIs are indispensable. They allow applications to access real-time stock market data, currency exchange rates, and even process transactions through secure payment gateways. Whether you're building a trading platform, a personal finance app, or a cryptocurrency tracker, financial APIs give you the tools to keep users informed and empowered.

- **AI APIs:** The realm of AI is vast and complex, but APIs make it accessible. Services like IBM Watson or OpenAI provide APIs that allow developers to integrate advanced AI capabilities into their applications. From natural language processing to image recognition, these APIs enable your app to perform tasks that would otherwise require deep expertise in machine learning.

In every corner of the digital world, APIs are the bridges that connect disparate systems, enabling them to work together in harmony. By mastering the art of API interaction, you unlock the potential to create applications that are not only functional but also deeply integrated with the digital ecosystem.

Data Formats in APIs

As you go into the API Abyss, you'll encounter different data formats that APIs use to communicate. Understanding these formats is crucial, as they determine how you will parse and utilize the data returned by an API.

JSON: The Treasure Map

JSON is the most commonly used data format in APIs. It's lightweight, easy to read, and supported by virtually all programming languages. JSON structures data in key-value pairs, making it easy to navigate and extract specific information.

Here's a typical JSON structure:

```
{
    "name": "John Doe",
    "age": 30,
    "city": "New York"
}
```

In Python, you can easily work with JSON data using the **json** module. Converting a JSON string into a Python dictionary is straightforward:

```
import json
```

```
json_string = '{"name": "John Doe", "age": 30, "city": "New York"}'
data = json.loads(json_string)
print(data['name'])  # Output: John Doe
```

Once you have the data in a Python dictionary, you can manipulate it as needed—adding, modifying, or removing elements:

```
data['email'] = 'johndoe@example.com'  # Adding a new key-value pair
data['age'] = 31                       # Modifying an existing value
del data['city']                       # Removing a key-value pair
```

If you need to send this modified data back to an API, you can convert it back to a JSON string:

```
modified_json = json.dumps(data)
print(modified_json)
```

XML: The Ancient Scrolls

While JSON is the modern standard, you may also encounter APIs that use XML (short for Extensible Markup Language). XML is more verbose than JSON and is structured in a hierarchical format with nested elements. It's often used in industries where data complexity and metadata are important, such as healthcare and finance.

Here's an example of XML data:

```
<person>
    <name>John Smith</name>
    <age>35</age>
    <address>
        <street>123 Main St</street>
        <city>New York</city>
        <state>NY</state>
        <zip>10001</zip>
    </address>
</person>
```

In Python, you can work with XML data using the **xml.etree.ElementTree** module. To parse XML data, start by converting it into an **ElementTree** object:

```
import xml.etree.ElementTree as ET

tree = ET.parse('data.xml')   # Parse an XML file
root = tree.getroot()         # Get the root element
print(root.tag)
```

With the root element in hand, you can navigate through the XML structure and extract the information you need:

```
for person in root.findall('person'):
    name = person.find('name').text
    age = person.find('age').text
    print(f'{name}, {age}')
```

You can also modify the XML data by adding, changing, or removing elements:

```
new_element = ET.SubElement(root, 'person')
new_element.set('name', 'Anna')

# Modifying an existing element
for person in root.findall('person'):
    if person.find('name').text == 'John Smith':
        person.find('name').text = 'Johnathan Smith'

# Removing an element
for person in root.findall('person'):
    if person.find('name').text == 'Jane Doe':
        root.remove(person)
```

Once you've made your changes, you can write the updated data back to an XML file or convert it to a string:

```
tree.write('modified_data.xml')   # Write to a file
xml_string = ET.tostring(root).decode()
print(xml_string)
```

Understanding the nuances between JSON and XML is essential. JSON is faster to process due to its lightweight nature, making it ideal for most API interactions. XML, while more complex, is useful for scenarios where data validation and metadata are crucial.

Introduction to Web Scraping

As you journey further into the API Abyss, you may find that not all data is readily accessible through APIs. Sometimes, the information you seek is locked away in the HTML of webpages. This is where web scraping comes into play—a technique that allows you to extract data directly from webpages by parsing their HTML structure.

Navigating the Web: The Art of Web Scraping

Web scraping is like diving into the deep ocean, where treasures lie hidden beneath the waves of HTML code. With the right tools, you can extract these treasures and bring them to the surface.

One of the most popular tools for web scraping in Python is the BeautifulSoup library. BeautifulSoup makes it easy to navigate and search through the HTML of webpages, allowing you to extract the data you need.

To begin your web scraping adventure, you'll need to install BeautifulSoup and the **requests** library:

```
pip install beautifulsoup4 requests
```

With your tools in hand, you can start writing your web scraping script. Begin by fetching the content of the webpage you wish to scrape:

```python
from bs4 import BeautifulSoup
import requests

url = 'https://example.com'
response = requests.get(url)
web_content = response.text
```

With the webpage content stored in the **web_content** variable, you can create a BeautifulSoup object to parse the HTML:

```python
soup = BeautifulSoup(web_content, 'html.parser')
```

Now, you can begin extracting data. For example, if you want to find all the headings (<h2> tags) on the page:

```
headings = soup.find_all('h2')
for heading in headings:
    print(heading.text)
```

You can extract other elements as well, such as paragraphs or list items, using their respective tags:

```
paragraphs = soup.find_all('p')
for paragraph in paragraphs:
  print(paragraph.text)
```

Navigating Ethically: The Code of Web Scraping

While web scraping is a powerful tool, it's important to practice it ethically. Always review and adhere to the terms of service of the website you're scraping. Check the **robots.txt** file of the target website to understand any restrictions or guidelines regarding web scraping.

It's also crucial to avoid overloading servers with too many requests, as this can lead to IP blocks or CAPTCHAs. Introducing delays between your requests is a good practice:

```
import time

for i in range(10):
    print(f"Fetching page {i}")
    time.sleep(2)  # sleep for 2 seconds
```

Diving Deeper: Practical Web Scraping Examples

Let's explore some practical examples of web scraping tasks. Suppose you want to scrape quotes and authors from a hypothetical quotes website. Here's how you can do it:

```
url = 'http://quotes.toscrape.com'
response = requests.get(url)
soup = BeautifulSoup(response.text, 'html.parser')

# Extract quotes
quotes = soup.find_all('span', class_='text')
authors = soup.find_all('small', class_='author')

for quote, author in zip(quotes, authors):
    print(f"{quote.text} - {author.text}")
```

This example demonstrates how to fetch a webpage, parse its HTML, and extract specific data points like quotes and their corresponding authors.

Another useful scenario might involve scraping product details from an ecommerce website. Consider the following script that extracts product names and prices:

```
url = 'https://example-ecommerce.com/products'
response = requests.get(url)
soup = BeautifulSoup(response.text, 'html.parser')

products = soup.find_all('div', class_='product')

for product in products:
    name = product.find('h3').text
    price = product.find('span', class_='price').text
    print(f"Product: {name}, Price: {price}")
```

This script showcases how you can retrieve specific information about products, which can be valuable for competitive analysis or inventory management.

Facing the Kraken: The Final Boss

Your journey through the API Abyss has prepared you for the ultimate challenge—the Data Kraken. This final boss represents the complexity of integrating multiple APIs, processing the data, and presenting it meaningfully to users.

To defeat the Data Kraken, you must create a web application or script that integrates data from various sources, processes it, and presents it in a user-friendly format.

Imagine you're tasked with building a travel planning app. Your app needs to integrate data from several APIs: one for flight information, another for hotel bookings, and a third for local attractions. The challenge lies not just in retrieving data from these APIs, but in merging and processing it in a way that makes sense to the user.

Assembling Your Arsenal: Integrating Multiple APIs

Start by identifying the APIs you need and understanding their endpoints, parameters, and response formats. For example, you might use the Skyscanner API for flight information, the Booking.com API for hotels, and the Yelp API for local attractions.

Begin by making requests to these APIs and handling their JSON responses:

```
import requests

# Fetch flight information
flights_response = requests.get('https://api.skyscanner.net/flights')
flights_data = flights_response.json()

# Fetch hotel information
hotels_response = requests.get('https://api.booking.com/hotels')
hotels_data = hotels_response.json()

# Fetch local attractions
attractions_response = requests.get('https://api.yelp.com/attractions')
attractions_data = attractions_response.json()
```

With the data retrieved, you'll need to process it—merging information, filtering based on user preferences, and sorting by relevance. This might involve complex data manipulations, such as combining flight and hotel availability based on dates and locations.

Building the Interface: Presenting Data to the User

Once the data is processed, the next step is to present it meaningfully to the user. This could involve creating a web interface where users can enter their travel preferences and receive customized travel plans.

Using Flask, a lightweight web framework in Python, you can create a user-friendly interface:

```
from flask import Flask, render_template, request

app = Flask(__name__)

@app.route('/')
def home():
    return render_template('index.html')

@app.route('/plan', methods=['POST'])
def plan():
    # Process user input and generate travel plan
    user_input = request.form
    # Integrate and process data from multiple APIs
    travel_plan = generate_travel_plan(user_input)
    return render_template('plan.html', plan=travel_plan)

def generate_travel_plan(user_input):
```

```
    # Placeholder function for processing API data
    return "Your customized travel plan."

if __name__ == '__main__':
    app.run(debug=True)
```

This Flask application allows users to input their preferences and receive a customized travel plan. Behind the scenes, your script fetches and processes data from multiple APIs, integrating it into a cohesive plan.

Tackling Authentication in APIs

Many APIs require secure access, which often involves handling authentication via API keys or OAuth. These methods ensure that only authorized users can access certain data or perform specific actions.

- **API keys:** The simplest form of authentication is the API key, which is typically passed as a query parameter or in the request header. Here's an example of how to use an API key in a request:

```
headers = {
    'Authorization': 'Bearer YOUR_API_KEY'
}
response = requests.get('https://api.example.com/data', headers=headers)
```

- **OAuth:** OAuth is a more secure and complex authentication method, often used by APIs that require user permissions. It involves obtaining a token that represents the user's authorization. Handling OAuth requires careful management of tokens and secrets. Here's a basic example using OAuth with the requests-oauthlib library:

```
pip install requests-oauthlib

from requests_oauthlib import OAuth1Session

# Replace these values with your application's credentials
client_key = 'your_client_key'
client_secret = 'your_client_secret'
resource_owner_key = 'your_resource_owner_key'
resource_owner_secret = 'your_resource_owner_secret'

oauth = OAuth1Session(client_key, client_secret=client_secret,
                      resource_owner_key=resource_owner_key,
                      resource_owner_secret=resource_owner_secret)
```

```
response = oauth.get('https://api.example.com/resource')
print(response.json())
```

Handling authentication securely is crucial for protecting sensitive data and ensuring that your application complies with the API provider's usage policies.

Advanced Error Handling and Status Code Management

APIs can return a variety of status codes, each indicating a different outcome. While handling a successful response is straightforward, managing errors requires a robust approach.

- **Handling rate limits: Many APIs enforce rate limits to prevent abuse.** When a rate limit is exceeded, the API will return a status code like 429 (Too Many Requests). Implementing a retry mechanism with exponential backoff is a common strategy:

```python
import time

def fetch_data_with_retry(url, headers):
    for i in range(5):
        response = requests.get(url, headers=headers)
        if response.status_code == 200:
            return response.json()
        elif response.status_code == 429:
            time.sleep(2 ** i)  # Exponential backoff
        else:
            response.raise_for_status()

# Usage
data = fetch_data_with_retry('https://api.example.com/data', headers)
```

- **Handling timeouts and network errors:** Network conditions are not always stable. Implementing timeout handling and retry logic can help your application remain resilient:

```python
try:
    response = requests.get('https://api.example.com/data', timeout=5)
    response.raise_for_status()  # Raises an HTTPError if the status code is not
200
    data = response.json()
except requests.exceptions.Timeout:
    print("The request timed out")
```

```
except requests.exceptions.RequestException as e:
    print(f"An error occurred: {e}")
```

Being prepared to handle various types of errors ensures that your application can recover gracefully from unexpected issues.

Tackling XML Parsing and Manipulation

The section on XML parsing can be expanded by introducing more advanced techniques, such as handling namespaces or using XPath to navigate XML documents.

- **Handling namespaces:** Some XML documents use namespaces, which can make parsing a bit tricky. Here's how to handle namespaces with ElementTree:

```
import xml.etree.ElementTree as ET

tree = ET.parse('data.xml')
root = tree.getroot()

# Register namespaces
namespaces = {'ns': 'http://www.example.com/ns'}
for elem in root.findall('ns:person', namespaces):
    name = elem.find('ns:name', namespaces).text
    print(name)
```

- Using XPath: XPath allows you to select nodes in an XML document more flexibly:

```
# Find all person elements where the age is greater than 30
persons = root.findall(".//person[age>30]")
for person in persons:
    name = person.find('name').text
    print(name)
```

These advanced techniques are useful when dealing with complex XML documents, especially those that are common in industries like healthcare and finance.

More Advanced Web Scraping Techniques

As web technologies evolve, so too must your web scraping techniques. Modern websites often rely on JavaScript to load content dynamically, which requires more advanced tools like Selenium for scraping.

- Using Selenium for JavaScript-heavy websites:

```
pip install selenium

from selenium import webdriver

# Set up the WebDriver
driver = webdriver.Chrome()

# Open the webpage
driver.get('https://example.com')

# Wait for elements to load and interact with them
heading = driver.find_element_by_tag_name('h1')
print(heading.text)

# Close the driver
driver.quit()
```

Selenium allows you to interact with web pages in real time, making it possible to scrape content that would otherwise be inaccessible using standard requests.

Handling API Rate Limiting and Pagination

APIs often paginate their results, requiring you to handle multiple requests to retrieve all the data. Here's how to manage pagination:

- Handling pagination:

```
url = 'https://api.example.com/data'
params = {'page': 1}
all_data = []

while True:
    response = requests.get(url, params=params)
    data = response.json()
    all_data.extend(data['results'])

    if not data['next']:  # Check if there's a next page
        break

    params['page'] += 1
```

```
print(f"Retrieved {len(all_data)} records")
```

- Handling rate limiting:

As discussed earlier, handling rate limiting involves implementing a retry mechanism with exponential backoff to respect the API's constraints.

Expanding the Flask Example

The Flask example provided earlier can be expanded to handle form submissions, work with sessions, and even deploy the application to a platform like Heroku.

- Handling form submissions:

```
from flask import Flask, render_template, request, redirect, url_for

app = Flask(__name__)

@app.route('/')
def index():
    return render_template('index.html')

@app.route('/submit', methods=['POST'])
def submit():
    data = request.form
    return redirect(url_for('result', name=data['name']))

@app.route('/result/<name>')
def result(name):
    return f"Hello, {name}!"

if __name__ == '__main__':
    app.run(debug=True)
```

- Deploying to Heroku:

To deploy this Flask application to Heroku, you would need to create a **Procfile** and a **requirements.txt** file, and use the Heroku CLI to push your code:

```
heroku create
git push heroku master
heroku open
```

By expanding on these features, you can create a more complex and fully functional web application.

Your journey through the API Abyss has taken you from the basics of making API calls to the complexities of integrating multiple data sources and presenting them in a meaningful way. Along the way, you've learned to navigate the challenges of web scraping, handle different data formats, and use regular expressions to manipulate text data.

But most importantly, you've faced the ultimate challenge—integrating APIs to create a functional, user-friendly application—and emerged victorious. The skills you've gained will serve you well as you continue to explore the depths of software development, unlocking new possibilities and creating powerful, integrated applications.

The API Abyss is vast and ever-changing, but with the knowledge and tools you now possess, you are ready to navigate its waters with confidence and creativity. Whether you're building applications that connect to social media, financial services, or advanced AI models, the power of APIs is at your fingertips, waiting to be unleashed.

CHAPTER 11

The Final Fortress

Integrating all Python skills to overcome the ultimate challenge is a matter of synthesizing what you've learned into one final, formidable task. Now you're standing before an imposing fortress. Each stone symbolizes the countless hours spent mastering variables, loops, data structures, and APIs. The Final Fortress isn't just a physical barrier but a grand stage where theory meets practice, testing your knowledge at every turn. As you approach closer, its towering ramparts and designed gates reveal that every step you've taken has led you here. This is the place where each piece of code, each snippet of logic, comes together for one final showdown.

In this final chapter, you'll go into how all your Python skills integrate to overcome such an enormous challenge. From basic syntax to complex algorithms, the journey through the fortress will demand an application of everything you've learned. You'll navigate rooms filled with puzzles involving list comprehensions, dictionaries, and OOP. You'll harness the power of file handling and API interactions, applying them in sophisticated ways to tackle real-time data problems. Are you ready? Let's begin.

Exploring the Fortress

Inside the Final Fortress, the challenges are relentless, pushing you to your limits. Each room or chamber within the fortress could be seen as representing different Python topics. One might be filled with puzzles involving list comprehensions and dictionaries, while another challenges you to harness the power of object-oriented principles to create sophisticated class hierarchies.

Challenge 1: List Comprehensions and Dictionaries

One of the first rooms you enter in the Final Fortress presents a puzzle involving list comprehensions and dictionaries. The task is to transform and filter a dataset efficiently. Here's a challenge: Given a list of dictionaries representing employees, create a new list that contains only the names of employees who are active and have a salary above a certain threshold.

```python
employees = [
    {"name": "Alice", "active": True, "salary": 70000},
    {"name": "Bob", "active": False, "salary": 50000},
    {"name": "Charlie", "active": True, "salary": 120000},
    {"name": "Diana", "active": True, "salary": 80000},          .
]

threshold = 75000
active_high_earners = [emp["name"] for emp in employees if emp["active"] and
emp["salary"] > threshold]

print(active_high_earners)  # Output: ['Charlie', 'Diana']
```

This room tests your ability to combine logical conditions with list comprehensions, a powerful Pythonic tool.

Challenge 2: OOP

Moving to another chamber, you are required to demonstrate mastery of OOP. The challenge is to create a simple simulation of a library system where books can be borrowed and returned. Implement classes for **Book**, **Library**, and **Member**, ensuring that the library can manage its inventory and track which books are checked out by which members.

```python
class Book:
    def __init__(self, title, author):
        self.title = title
        self.author = author
        self.borrowed = False

    def borrow(self):
        if not self.borrowed:
            self.borrowed = True
            return True
        return False
```

```python
    def return_book(self):
        if self.borrowed:
            self.borrowed = False
            return True
        return False

class Member:
    def __init__(self, name):
        self.name = name
        self.borrowed_books = []

    def borrow_book(self, book):
        if book.borrow():
            self.borrowed_books.append(book)
            print(f"{self.name} borrowed {book.title}")
        else:
            print(f"{book.title} is already borrowed")

    def return_book(self, book):
        if book in self.borrowed_books:
            if book.return_book():
                self.borrowed_books.remove(book)
                print(f"{self.name} returned {book.title}")

class Library:
    def __init__(self, books):
        self.books = books

    def available_books(self):
        return [book.title for book in self.books if not book.borrowed]

# Example usage
books = [Book("The Great Gatsby", "F. Scott Fitzgerald"), Book("1984", "George Orwell")]
library = Library(books)
member = Member("John Doe")

member.borrow_book(books[0])
print("Available books:", library.available_books())

member.return_book(books[0])
print("Available books:", library.available_books())
```

This challenge solidifies your understanding of how to design classes that interact with each other, manage states, and encapsulate logic.

Challenge 3: File Handling

Next, you enter a chamber that tests your ability to handle files. You're asked to write a Python script that reads a CSV file containing customer orders and generates a summary report that groups the orders by customer and calculates the total amount spent by each customer.

```python
import csv

def summarize_orders(filename):
    orders_summary = {}
    with open(filename, mode='r') as file:
        reader = csv.DictReader(file)
        for row in reader:
            customer = row['Customer']
            amount = float(row['Amount'])
            if customer in orders_summary:
                orders_summary[customer] += amount
            else:
                orders_summary[customer] = amount

    return orders_summary

# Example usage
summary = summarize_orders('orders.csv')
for customer, total in summary.items():
    print(f"{customer}: ${total:.2f}")
```

This task reinforces your ability to work with external data sources, process the data efficiently, and generate meaningful reports.

Challenge 4: API Integration

One of the final chambers requires you to interact with an external API. The challenge is to build a script that fetches real-time weather data for a list of cities and then saves the results to a JSON file. You'll use Python's **requests** library to make API calls and handle JSON data.

```python
import requests
import json
```

```python
def fetch_weather(city):
    api_key = "your_api_key"
    url =
f"http://api.openweathermap.org/data/2.5/weather?q={city}&appid={api_key}&units=metric"
    response = requests.get(url)
    if response.status_code == 200:
        return response.json()
    else:
        return None

def save_weather_data(cities, filename):
    weather_data = {}
    for city in cities:
        data = fetch_weather(city)
        if data:
            weather_data[city] = data['main']
        else:
            weather_data[city] = "Data not available"

    with open(filename, 'w') as file:
        json.dump(weather_data, file, indent=4)

# Example usage
cities = ["London", "New York", "Tokyo"]
save_weather_data(cities, 'weather_data.json')
```

This exercise demonstrates your proficiency in working with APIs, handling JSON data, and saving results in a structured format.

The Penultimate Challenge

The road ahead is a formidable one, combining all the skills you've acquired to tackle an intricate grand project. This final challenge represents the synthesis of your learning journey. If you put together variables, loops, data structures, OOP, file handling, and API integrations, you will demonstrate not only your technical prowess but also your ability to weave together diverse elements into a cohesive solution.

Integrated Final Project

Imagine you are tasked with developing a comprehensive system that combines everything you've learned. For instance, build a project that manages a small ecommerce platform. The system should allow users to browse products, place orders, and manage their account details. This project would require a combination of all the skills mentioned:

1. **Data structures and OOP:** Use classes to model products, orders, and users.

2. **File handling:** Store user and order information in CSV or JSON files.

3. **API integration:** Use an external API to process payments or retrieve product data.

4. **Loops and conditionals:** Implement the logic for navigating menus, processing user input, and managing the shopping cart.

Here's a simplified structure to get you started:

```python
import json
import requests

class Product:
    def __init__(self, name, price):
        self.name = name
        self.price = price

class User:
    def __init__(self, username, balance):
        self.username = username
        self.balance = balance
        self.cart = []

    def add_to_cart(self, product):
        self.cart.append(product)
        print(f"{product.name} added to cart")

    def checkout(self):
        total = sum(product.price for product in self.cart)
        if total > self.balance:
            print("Insufficient balance")
        else:
            self.balance -= total
            print("Purchase successful!")
            self.cart.clear()

class ECommercePlatform:
```

```python
    def __init__(self, products, users):
        self.products = products
        self.users = users

    def display_products(self):
        for product in self.products:
            print(f"{product.name}: ${product.price}")

    def user_login(self, username):
        for user in self.users:
            if user.username == username:
                return user
        print("User not found")
        return None

# Example usage
products = [Product("Laptop", 999.99), Product("Smartphone", 499.99)]
users = [User("JohnDoe", 1500.00)]

platform = ECommercePlatform(products, users)
platform.display_products()

user = platform.user_login("JohnDoe")
if user:
    user.add_to_cart(products[0])
    user.checkout()
```

Bugzilla: The Ultimate Challenge

In every programmer's journey through Pythonia, there's a nemesis that haunts them, lurking in the shadows of their code, waiting for the right moment to strike. This adversary is not a villain in the traditional sense, but rather a reflection of the coder's growing pains—an embodiment of every error, every bug, every unexpected behavior that disrupts the smooth flow of a program. This is Bugzilla, the great and terrible creature that you must face in the Final Fortress.

Bugzilla didn't start as a monstrous beast. Early in your coding journey, it might have been a small, pesky creature—an unexpected syntax error or a simple logic flaw. Back then, you might have squashed these bugs without much effort, perhaps even with a sense of accomplishment. But as you continued facing the complexities of Python, Bugzilla began to grow. Its form became more twisted, more chaotic, symbolizing the increasing difficulty and intricacy of the problems you were encountering.

At first, Bugzilla might have been a minor annoyance, like a missing colon or a misspelled variable name:

```
# An example of a small bug - syntax error
def say_hello()
    print("Hello, world!")
```

Here, Bugzilla might have appeared as a small gremlin, easily defeated by adding the missing colon after the function definition:

```
def say_hello():
    print("Hello, world!")
```

But as your projects grew in complexity, Bugzilla evolved. It became a more formidable opponent, representing bugs that were harder to identify and more challenging to fix. These weren't just syntax errors—they were logical errors, race conditions, or even performance bottlenecks. Here's an example of a more complex bug:

```
# A more complex bug - logical error
def calculate_discount(price, discount):
    final_price = price - (price * discount / 100)
    if final_price < 0:
        return "Invalid discount!"
    return final_price

# Testing the function
print(calculate_discount(100, 120))  # Output: "Invalid discount!"
```

On the surface, the code seems to work fine. But Bugzilla lurks here, revealing its presence when you realize that allowing a discount greater than 100% isn't realistic, yet the function doesn't handle it properly. You can fix this by adding a check for the discount percentage:

```
def calculate_discount(price, discount):
    if discount > 100 or discount < 0:
        return "Invalid discount!"
    final_price = price - (price * discount / 100)
    return final_price

# Testing the function
print(calculate_discount(100, 120))  # Output: "Invalid discount!"
```

Facing Bugzilla: The Battle Begins

As you progress through the Final Fortress, Bugzilla's presence grows stronger, manifesting in more insidious ways. Imagine you're working on a project that involves processing large datasets. Bugzilla might appear as a memory leak or a performance issue, slowing down your program to a crawl. Here's an example:

```python
# A memory issue example
def create_large_list(size):
    large_list = []
    for i in range(size):
        large_list.append("Item " + str(i))
    return large_list


# Testing with a large size
large_list = create_large_list(10**6)
```

At first glance, this code might seem fine, but Bugzilla whispers in the background, pointing out that the list is growing too large, consuming a lot of memory. One way to battle this form of Bugzilla is to rethink your approach. Perhaps using a generator instead of a list might help:

```python
# Using a generator to handle large data more efficiently
def create_large_list(size):
    for i in range(size):
        yield "Item " + str(i)


# Using the generator
for item in create_large_list(10**6):
    print(item)
```

This approach helps manage memory more efficiently, as items are generated on the fly rather than stored in memory.

As you continue to face Bugzilla, the challenges become even more complex. Perhaps now you're dealing with a multithreaded application, and Bugzilla reveals itself as a race condition—a situation where the timing of thread execution causes unpredictable behavior:

```python
import threading


# A race condition example
```

```python
counter = 0

def increment():
    global counter
    for _ in range(100000):
        counter += 1

# Creating two threads
thread1 = threading.Thread(target=increment)
thread2 = threading.Thread(target=increment)

# Starting the threads
thread1.start()
thread2.start()

# Waiting for threads to finish
thread1.join()
thread2.join()

print(counter)  # Expected output: 200000, but might be less due to the race
condition
```

In this battle, Bugzilla takes on a chaotic form, reflecting the unpredictable nature of race conditions. The fix involves using a lock to ensure that only one thread modifies the counter at a time:

```python
import threading

# Fixing the race condition with a lock
counter = 0
lock = threading.Lock()

def increment():
    global counter
    for _ in range(100000):
        with lock:
            counter += 1

# Creating and starting the threads
thread1 = threading.Thread(target=increment)
thread2 = threading.Thread(target=increment)

thread1.start()
thread2.start()
```

```
thread1.join()
thread2.join()

print(counter)  # Output should consistently be 200000
```

Activities to Defeat Bugzilla

Throughout your journey in the Final Fortress, you'll face different forms of Bugzilla. Here are some activities that will help you defeat this formidable foe:

1. **Identify and fix syntax errors:**

    o **Task:** Write a function with deliberate syntax errors. Identify and correct them.

    o **Example:**

```
def greet(name):
    print(f"Hello, {name}!)Fix:def greet(name):
    print(f"Hello, {name}!")
```

2. **Debug logical errors:**

    o **Task:** Create a function with a logical error. Use print statements or debugging tools to find and fix it.

    o **Example:**

```
def find_max(numbers):
    max_num = 0  # Logical error: This assumes numbers are all positive
    for num in numbers:
        if num > max_num:
            max_num = num
    return max_num
```

    o Fix:

```
def find_max(numbers):
    max_num = numbers[0]
    for num in numbers:
        if num > max_num:
```

```
        max_num = num
    return max_num
```

3. Manage memory efficiently:

- o **Task:** Refactor a function that uses too much memory. Consider using generators or other memory-efficient techniques.

- o Example:

```
def create_list(size):
    return [i for i in range(size)]
```

- o Refactor:

```
def create_list(size):
    for i in range(size):
        yield i
```

4. Resolve race conditions:

- o **Task:** Implement a multithreaded program with a race condition and then fix it using locks.

- o Example:

```
import threading

def update_shared_resource():
    # Simulated race condition
    pass
```

5. Fix:

```
import threading

lock = threading.Lock()

def update_shared_resource():
    with lock:
```

```
    # Safe access to shared resource
    pass
```

The Redemption Arc: Bugzilla Transformed

After countless battles, you finally reach the heart of the Final Fortress, where Bugzilla awaits. But as you prepare for the final strike, something unexpected happens. Bugzilla doesn't resist—instead, it begins to transform. You realize that Bugzilla wasn't just a monster to be defeated but a teacher, guiding you through the complexities of coding.

Bugzilla starts to shrink, its chaotic form becoming more ordered and even helpful. This transformation symbolizes your mastery over debugging and your growth as a programmer. Bugzilla is no longer the fearsome creature that haunted your early coding days; it's now a wise guide, representing the deep understanding you've gained about code, logic, and problem-solving.

Here's a final activity to symbolize Bugzilla's transformation:

- **Activity: Embrace debugging:**
  - **Task:** Deliberately introduce a complex bug into your code. Then, using all the skills you've learned, debug the code. Reflect on the process—how did you approach the problem? What strategies did you use? Write a brief summary of your approach and the lessons learned.

  - **Example bug:**

```
def calculate_statistics(data):
    mean = sum(data) / len(data)
    median = data[len(data) // 2]  # This assumes the data is sorted
    mode = max(set(data), key=data.count)
    return mean, median, mode

data = [5, 1, 2, 2, 3, 4, 1, 5]
print(calculate_statistics(data))
```

  - **Debugging process:**

    - Realize the median calculation is incorrect because the data isn't sorted.

    - Implement a fix by sorting the data before calculating the median:

```python
def calculate_statistics(data):
    sorted_data = sorted(data)
    mean = sum(data) / len(data)
    median = sorted_data[len(sorted_data) // 2]
    mode = max(set(data), key=data.count)
    return mean, median, mode
```

You did it! You defeated the final challenge! As you exit the Final Fortress, you don't leave Bugzilla behind. Instead, you take it with you—not as an adversary, but as a symbol of your journey. Bugzilla, once a harbinger of frustration and error, now represents the growth, knowledge, and mastery you've gained. It reminds you that every bug, every error, every challenge is an opportunity to learn and improve.

With Bugzilla by your side, transformed into a guide and ally, you are now ready to face the world of programming with confidence and creativity. Every line of code, every project you undertake, will be a testament to your resilience, skill, and the lessons learned from your battles with Bugzilla.

Conclusion

As you stand at the edge of the fortress, it's time to reflect on the path you've walked, the skills you've honed, and the challenges you've conquered. The Final Fortress is behind you, Bugzilla has been redeemed, and the mysteries of Python have been unraveled one by one. But even as this journey concludes, a new one begins—an adventure filled with endless possibilities in the vast world of programming.

Take a moment to look around. The world of Pythonia, once a place of uncertainty and challenge, now feels like home. The towering walls of the Final Fortress that once loomed large and intimidating now stand as monuments to your resilience, each stone a testament to the countless hours you've dedicated to mastering the art of programming.

The sunset casts a golden hue over the landscape, symbolizing not just the end of a day but the culmination of your efforts. The air is thick with a sense of accomplishment, yet there's also a quiet anticipation—a whisper that this is only the beginning.

In the heart of Pythonia, Py and the Debugger gather to celebrate your achievements. The Guild's Hall is alive with joy and camaraderie, where every corner is adorned with symbols of the milestones you've reached. It's a place where knowledge and experience are celebrated, and where the hard work you've put in is recognized by those who have walked similar paths.

As you stand among your peers in the Guild's Hall, memories of your journey come flooding back. You remember the early days, when even the simplest tasks—like writing your first function—felt like monumental achievements. Those were the days when you learned to crawl in the world of Python, grappling with variables, loops, and conditionals. That first "Hello, World!" program seems so long ago, yet it was the spark that ignited this incredible journey.

As you moved forward, the challenges grew more complex, and so did your skills. You mastered the art of manipulating data structures, creating and managing lists, dictionaries, and sets with increasing finesse. The concepts of OOP, which once seemed abstract, became second nature to you, allowing you to model real-world scenarios with Python classes and objects.

You recall your initial struggles with APIs, where interacting with external systems felt like learning a new language. But with persistence, you learned to harness their power, opening doors to endless possibilities—whether it was pulling data from the web, automating tasks, or creating dynamic, responsive applications.

File handling was another significant milestone. You learned to read from and write to files, manage data efficiently, and ensure that your programs could interact with the world beyond the terminal. Each file opened, each line of data parsed, was a step toward mastering the art of coding.

And then, there was Bugzilla. The challenges Bugzilla represented were not just technical hurdles—they were lessons in perseverance, in the importance of debugging, and in the value of every mistake made along the way. Defeating Bugzilla wasn't just about fixing bugs; it was about embracing the challenges of coding and transforming frustration into mastery.

Now, as you reflect on your journey, it's clear how each key concept you learned played a vital role in your growth:

1. **Variables and data types:** These were your first tools, the building blocks of every program you wrote. From integers and strings to more complex data types like lists, dictionaries, and sets, you learned how to store and manipulate data, laying the foundation for everything that followed.

2. **Control flow:** Loops and conditionals gave you the power to control the flow of your programs, making them dynamic and responsive. You mastered **if-else** statements, **for** and **while** loops, and logical operators, enabling you to write code that could adapt to different situations.

3. **Functions and scope:** Functions became your way of organizing code, breaking down complex problems into manageable pieces. You learned the importance of scope, understanding how variables are accessed within different contexts, and how to write clean, efficient code.

4. **OOP:** As you went into OOP, you began to think in terms of objects and classes, modeling real-world entities in your programs. Inheritance, polymorphism, and encapsulation became second nature, allowing you to build sophisticated, reusable code structures.

5. **File handling:** The ability to read from and write to files opened up new possibilities, enabling you to create programs that could persist data beyond runtime. You learned how to interact with the file system, manage data storage, and build applications that are robust and user-friendly.

6. **APIs and web services:** Learning to interact with external systems through APIs was a gateway to a vast array of possibilities. You mastered the art of making HTTP requests, handling JSON data, and integrating third-party services into your projects.

7. **Debugging and testing:** Debugging became not just a skill, but an art. You learned to identify and fix bugs efficiently, using tools like **print** statements, debugging environments, and automated tests to ensure your code was reliable and robust.

8. **Libraries and modules:** Python's ecosystem of libraries and modules became your toolkit, enabling you to accomplish complex tasks with ease. From **numpy** and **pandas** for data manipulation to **matplotlib** for visualization, these tools empowered you to push the boundaries of what you could create.

As the celebration in the Guild's Hall begins to wind down, Py steps forward and addresses you directly. "You've come far," Py begins, "but the journey of learning never truly ends. The skills you've acquired are the keys to countless doors, but there are always more to unlock."

Py encourages you to continue exploring Python, to go deeper into areas that sparked your curiosity during this journey. "Perhaps you found joy in working with data—if so, consider exploring data science more fully. Libraries like **pandas**, **scikit-learn**, and **tensorflow** offer a wealth of tools for analyzing data, building machine learning models, and even delving into AI."

"For those who enjoyed creating dynamic, interactive applications, the world of web development awaits," Py continues. "Frameworks like Django and Flask can help you build robust, scalable web applications. And if automation caught your fancy, there's much more to explore in the realms of scripting and DevOps."

"Join coding communities, attend meetups, and contribute to open-source projects," Py advises. "The world of Python is vast, and by connecting with others, you'll continue to learn, grow, and share your knowledge with fellow programmers."

As you leave the Guild's Hall and step out into the world of Pythonia, remember that this journey was just the beginning. The skills you've gained, the challenges you've overcome, and the knowledge you've acquired are the foundation upon which you can build anything you dream of.

The world of programming is vast, full of new languages to learn, technologies to explore, and problems to solve. Keep pushing yourself, keep learning, and keep coding. The future is wide open, and with Python by your side, there's no limit to what you can achieve.

Celebrate your success, but know that the adventure never truly ends. The road ahead is filled with endless possibilities, and with each step, you'll continue to grow, to learn, and to create. So, go forth, explore, and let your journey in the world of programming be as boundless as your imagination.

References

Alphacozeop. (2024, May 17). *Loops in programming*. GeeksforGeeks. https://www.geeksforgeeks.org/loops-programming/

Are tuples more efficient than lists in Python? (n.d.). Stack Overflow. https://stackoverflow.com/questions/68630/are-tuples-more-efficient-than-lists-in-python

Arroyo, J. (2020, April 16). *On defense of "bad" variable names: Is GR really that bad*. Service Now Community. https://www.servicenow.com/community/developer-articles/on-defense-of-quot-bad-quot-variable-names-is-gr-really-that-bad/ta-p/2320632

ayushmaan bansal. (2024, September 02). *Python dictionary*. GeeksforGeeks. https://www.geeksforgeeks.org/python-dictionary/

Bhui, J. S. (2020, August 5). *Applying OOP in real world applications*. The Startup. https://medium.com/swlh/applying-oop-in-real-world-applications-495c8ee4d946

Bobyr, V. K. (2024). *Parsing a addition/subtraction/multiplication/division sign from a string*. Stack Overflow. https://stackoverflow.com/questions/38304945/parsing-a-addition-subtraction-multiplication-division-sign-from-a-string

Bonthu, H. (2021, August 21). *Python tutorial: Working with CSV file for data science*. Analytics Vidhya. https://www.analyticsvidhya.com/blog/2021/08/python-tutorial-working-with-csv-file-for-data-science/

Can a lambda function call itself recursively in Python? (2024). Stack Overflow. https://stackoverflow.com/questions/481692/can-a-lambda-function-call-itself-recursively-in-python

Castle symbolism. (2017, July 4). *myths symbols sandplay*. https://mythsymbolsandplay.typepad.com/my-blog/2017/07/castle-symbolism.html

C break and continue. (n.d.). W3Schools. https://www.w3schools.com/c/c_break_continue.php

Chan, A. (2021, December 8). *Follow these patterns to untangle your nested if statements*. Medium. https://lawyerdev.medium.com/i-never-write-nested-ifs-e4e91a5440ee

Chatterjee, A. (2024, June 17). Effective error handling strategies in automated tests. *TestRigor*. https://testrigor.com/blog/error-handling-strategies-in-automated-tests/

Codemotion. (2024, June 24). *Common mistakes in code reviews and how to avoid them*. https://www.codemotion.com/magazine/dev-life/common-mistakes-in-code-reviews-and-how-to-avoid-them/

Cook, A. (n.d.). *Arithmetic and variables*. Kaggle. https://www.kaggle.com/code/alexisbcook/arithmetic-and-variables

CSV — CSV file reading and writing — Python 3.8.1 documentation. (2020). Python.org. https://docs.python.org/3/library/csv.html

DataCamp Team. (n.d.). *if...elif...else in Python tutorial*. DataCamp. https://www.datacamp.com/tutorial/elif-statements-python*Data visualisation in Python using Matplotlib and Seaborn*. (2020, October 30). GeeksforGeeks. https://www.geeksforgeeks.org/data-visualisation-in-python-using-matplotlib-and-seaborn/

Data visualization in Python: Overview, libraries & graphs (n.d.). Simplilearn. https://www.simplilearn.com/tutorials/python-tutorial/data-visualization-in-python

Dhameja, S. (2024, June 18). *Continue statement in C: What is break & continue statement in C with example*. ScholarHat. https://www.scholarhat.com/tutorial/c/break-continue-statement-in-c

Custer, C. (2024, March 19). Python API tutorial: Getting started with APIs. *Dataquest*. https://www.dataquest.io/blog/python-api-tutorial/

The double-edged sword of inheritance: Weighing the advantages and disadvantages. (2024, April 27). *30DayCoding*. https://30dayscoding.com/blog/advantages-and-disadvantages-of-inheritance

5 phases of project management process (2023, April 15). Kissflow. https://kissflow.com/project/five-phases-of-project-management/

Fulkerson, J. (2021, September 14). *Looping vs iteration in JavaScript: A beginners guide to navigating both.* Geek Culture. https://medium.com/geekculture/looping-vs-iteration-in-javascript-a-beginners-guide-to-navigating-both-571ecdfd9cfe

Galarnyk, M., & Whitfield, B. (2023, August 11). *Python lists and list manipulation tutorial.* Built In. https://builtin.com/data-science/python-list

Gillis, A. S., & Lewis, S. (2024, June). *What is object-oriented programming (OOP)?* TechTarget App Architecture. https://www.techtarget.com/searchapparchitecture/definition/object-oriented-programming-OOP

Great Learning Editorial Team. (2023, June 26). else if Python: Understanding the nested conditional statements - 2024. *Great Learning Blog.* https://www.mygreatlearning.com/blog/else-if-python/

Hashemi-Pour, C., Brush, K., & Burns, E. (2024, August). *What is data visualization and why is it important?* TechTarget Business Analytics. https://www.techtarget.com/searchbusinessanalytics/definition/data-visualization

Hendawy, M. (2023, July 10). *Polymorphism in object-oriented programming with examples in C#.* Medium. https://mohamed-hendawy.medium.com/polymorphism-in-object-oriented-programming-with-examples-in-c-7329499cc706

How can I remove a key from a Python dictionary? (n.d.). Stack Overflow. https://stackoverflow.com/questions/11277432/how-can-i-remove-a-key-from-a-python-dictionary

IEEE Computer Society SBC of IIT. (2024, February 23). *Fundamentals of classes and objects in OOP.* Medium. https://medium.com/@ieeecomputersocietyiit/fundamentals-of-classes-and-objects-in-oop-5ac3b8a25bf1

Inheritance in Java. (2017, March 23). GeeksforGeeks. https://www.geeksforgeeks.org/inheritance-in-java/

Jain, P. (2023, June 13). *Encapsulation in Java: Understanding its importance and benefits.* JavaToDev. https://medium.com/spring-boot/encapsulation-in-java-understanding-its-importance-and-benefits-7009f03d557e

Jerline. (2023, June 18). Different techniques of debugging Selenium based test scripts. *Pcloudy*. https://www.pcloudy.com/blogs/different-techniques-of-debugging-selenium-based-test-scripts/

Joel. (2024). *Can I debug with Python debugger when using py.test somehow?* Stack Overflow. https://stackoverflow.com/questions/2678792/can-i-debug-with-python-debugger-when-using-py-test-somehow

Joukovsky, A. N. (2021, February 24). *Delusions of grandeur*. The Common. https://www.thecommononline.org/delusions-of-grandeur/

jwasham. (2024). *A complete computer science study plan to become a software engineer*. GitHub. https://github.com/jwasham/coding-interview-university

Kamah, D. (2021, April 12). *Variables are containers for storing data values*. Medium. https://kamah.medium.com/variables-are-containers-for-storing-data-values-1b727466b4f3

Kaubrė, V. (2023. May 8). *Python syntax errors: A guide to common mistakes and solutions*. Oxylabs. https://oxylabs.io/blog/python-syntax-errors

Mastering Python iterate dictionary: A comprehensive guide. (2020, July 9). EDUCBA. https://www.educba.com/python-iterate-dictionary/

Master modifying Python dictionaries - Add, update, delete key-value pairs. (2021). Llego. https://llego.dev/posts/master-modifying-python-dictionaries-add-update-delete-key-value-pairs/

Mirakyan, M. (2023, April). *Working with XML and JSON data in Python (90/100 days of Python)*. Medium. https://martinxpn.medium.com/working-with-xml-and-json-data-in-python-90-100-days-of-python-92b9a43672fd

mocopera. (2024). *How can I scrape a page with dynamic content (created by JavaScript) in Python?* Stack Overflow. https://stackoverflow.com/questions/8049520/how-can-i-scrape-a-page-with-dynamic-content-created-by-javascript-in-python

More control flow tools — Python 3.8.3 documentation. (n.d.). Python.org. https://docs.python.org/3/tutorial/controlflow.html

Navone, E. C. (2020, November 13). *Python while loop tutorial – While true syntax examples and infinite loops*. freeCodeCamp. https://www.freecodecamp.org/news/python-while-loop-tutorial/

Neufeld, R. (2024, January 19). *Debugging your unit test suite in Python*. Capital One.
https://www.capitalone.com/tech/software-engineering/how-to-use-python-debugger-pdb/

nikhilaggarwal3. (2024, 30 July). *Introduction to Pandas in Python*. GeeksforGeeks.
https://www.geeksforgeeks.org/introduction-to-pandas-in-python/

No runtime error after divison by zero. (n.d.). Stack Overflow.
https://stackoverflow.com/questions/29376100/no-runtime-error-after-divison-by-zero

Obregon, A. (2024, May 27). *Understanding API requests with Python*. Medium.
https://medium.com/@AlexanderObregon/working-with-apis-in-python-762f68938b16

Odhabi, H. (2018, September 29). *CIS 1403 lab 2 - Data types and variables*. Slideshare.
https://www.slideshare.net/slideshow/cis-1403-lab-2-data-types-and-variables/117267850

Ogabi, K. (2023, April 4). *Applying the DRY principle in software development*. Medium.
https://medium.com/@kefasogabi/applying-the-dry-principle-in-software-development-
28ad5376a9ae

Oluwadamisi, S. (2023, October 10). *Web scraping with BeautifulSoup: An in-depth guide for beginners*.
Medium. https://medium.com/@oluwadamisi.samuel/web-scraping-with-beautifulsoup-an-in-depth-
guide-for-beginners-412cb7826968

Oluwadamisi, S. (2024, January 30). *How to use Pandas for data cleaning and preprocessing*. FreeCodeCamp.
https://www.freecodecamp.org/news/data-cleaning-and-preprocessing-with-pandasbdvhj/

Pattern matching using regular expressions. (2024). Square-9. https://knowledge.square-
9.com/gc230/pattern-matching-using-regular-expressions

Paul-Afodi, D. (2022, September 8). Regular expressions and input validation. *OpenReplay*.
https://blog.openreplay.com/regular-expressions-and-input-validations/

pranathibadugu. (2024, July 24). *Python functions*. GeeksforGeeks. https://www.geeksforgeeks.org/python-
functions/

Premmaurya. (2019, June 17). *Polymorphism in Java*. GeeksforGeeks.
https://www.geeksforgeeks.org/polymorphism-in-java/

Project planning. (2022). ProjectManager. https://www.projectmanager.com/guides/project-planning

Python if, if...else, if...elif...else and nested if statement. (2019). Programiz. https://www.programiz.com/python-programming/if-elif-else

Python type conversion and type casting (with examples). (n.d.). Programiz.com. https://www.programiz.com/python-programming/type-conversion-and-casting

Python web-scraping. (2020). GitHub. https://iqss.github.io/dss-workshops/PythonWebScrape.html

Ramuglia, G. (2023, September 12). Python nested dictionary guide (with examples). *Linux Dedicated Server Blog.* https://ioflood.com/blog/python-nested-dictionary/

Recursion or iteration? (n.d.). Stack Overflow. https://stackoverflow.com/questions/72209/recursion-or-iteration

Recursive and lambda functions in Python. (2021, April 21). Dot Net Tutorials. https://dotnettutorials.net/lesson/recursive-and-lambda-functions-in-python/

Rind, A. (2024). *Python - Which is faster to parse JSON or XML?* Stack Overflow. https://stackoverflow.com/questions/7818030/python-which-is-faster-to-parse-json-or-xml

Riyana, J. (2021, September 7). *OOP concepts with real-world examples.* Medium. https://jeemariyana.medium.com/oop-concepts-with-real-world-examples-cda1cd277f4f

Rohittopi474. (2024, August 13). *Operations on sets.* GeeksforGeeks. https://www.geeksforgeeks.org/operations-on-sets/

Rosidi, N. (2023, July 20). Python dictionaries: Master key-value data structures. *StrataScratch.* https://www.stratascratch.com/blog/python-dictionaries-master-key-value-data-structures/

Sarker, I. H. (2021). *D*ata science and analytics: An overview from data-driven smart computing, decision-making and applications perspective. *SN Computer Science 2,* 377. https://doi.org/10.1007/s42979-021-00765-8

Set operations. (2024, August 27). GeeksforGeeks. https://www.geeksforgeeks.org/set-operations/

shivalibhadaniya. (2024, August 9). *Python3 - if , if..else, nested if, if-elif statements.* GeeksforGeeks. https://www.geeksforgeeks.org/python3-if-if-else-nested-if-if-elif-statements/

Simple calculations: Programming basics with Python. (n.d.). SoftUni Global. https://python-book.softuni.org/chapter-02-simple-calculations.html

Singh, V. K. (n.d.-a). BeautifulSoup web scraping guide. *Bright Data.* https://brightdata.com/blog/how-tos/beautiful-soup-web-scraping

Singh, V. K. (n.d.-b). How to build API integrations in Python. (2023, October 4). *Merge.* https://www.merge.dev/blog/api-integration-python

Sturtz, J. (2018, August 6). *Dictionaries in Python.* Real Python. https://realpython.com/python-dicts/

Time management strategies and tips. (n.d.). Atlassian. https://www.atlassian.com/work-management/project-management/time-management

Tiwari, N. (2024, June 20). *Data cleaning using Pandas in Python.* Analytics Vidhya. https://www.analyticsvidhya.com/blog/2021/06/data-cleaning-using-pandas/

Ulili, S. (2023, December 8). *15 common errors in Python and how to fix them.* Better Stack. https://betterstack.com/community/guides/scaling-python/python-errors/

Upadhyay, A. (2023, March 19). *Pandas functions for data cleaning, statistical analysis, EDA, and data visualization.* Medium. https://medium.com/@akriti.upadhyay/pandas-functions-for-data-cleaning-statistical-analysis-eda-and-data-visualization-f0d3abd53e61

Wei, L. (2024, April 29). *Understanding Python: The immutable tuple.* SQL Pad. https://sqlpad.io/tutorial/understanding-python-the-immutable-tuple/

What are the pros and cons in use of global variables? (2023). Stack Overflow. https://stackoverflow.com/questions/484635/what-are-the-pros-and-cons-in-use-of-global-variables

What is a variable in computer programming? (2019). LaunchSchool. https://launchschool.com/books/ruby/read/variables

What is encapsulation in OOP? (n.d.). Sumo Logic. https://www.sumologic.com/glossary/encapsulation/

What is iteration? (2021). Lenovo. https://www.lenovo.com/us/en/glossary/what-is-iteration/

While loop in C: Differences, infinite loop, examples. (2019). Vaia. https://www.vaia.com/en-us/explanations/computer-science/computer-programming/while-loop-in-c/

Why are nested loops considered bad practice? (2013, May 23). Software Engineering Stack Exchange. https://softwareengineering.stackexchange.com/questions/199196/why-are-nested-loops-considered-bad-practice

Why is DRY important? (2011, August 24). Software Engineering Stack Exchange. https://softwareengineering.stackexchange.com/questions/103233/why-is-dry-important

02DCE. (2024, June 24). *Phases of project management process.* GeeksforGeeks. https://www.geeksforgeeks.org/phases-project-management-processes/

Made in United States
Orlando, FL
31 October 2024